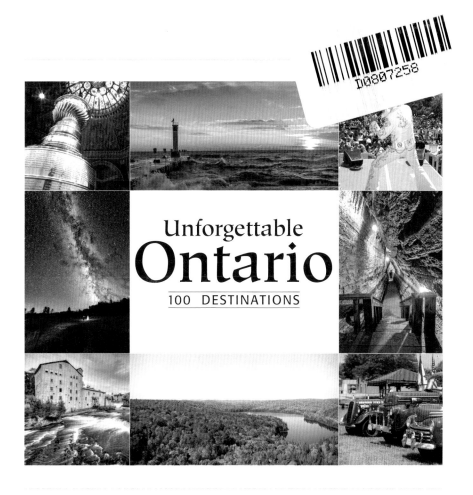

Unforgettable
Ontario
100 DESTINATIONS

Unforgettable
Ontario

100 DESTINATIONS

Noel Hudson

FIREFLY BOOKS

A Firefly Book

For John Denison

Published by Firefly Books Ltd. 2018
Copyright © 2018 Firefly Books Ltd.
Text copyright © 2018 Noel Hudson
Photographs © as listed on pages 254–255

First printing

Library of Congress Control Number: 2017961452

Library and Archives Canada Cataloguing in Publication
Hudson, Noel, 1956-, author
    Unforgettable Ontario : 100 destinations / Noel Hudson.

Includes biographical references and index.
ISBN 978-0-228-10025-6 (softcover)

    1. Ontario--Guidebooks. 2. Guidebooks. I. Title.

FC3057.H83 2018   917.1304'5   C2017-907469-5

Published in the United States by
Firefly Books (U.S.) Inc.
P.O. Box 1338, Ellicott Station
Buffalo, New York 14205

Published in Canada by
Firefly Books Ltd.
50 Staples Avenue, Unit 1
Richmond Hill, Ontario L4B 0A7

Original design by Gillian Stead/Adapted by Janice McLean
Printed in China

Canada

We acknowledge the financial support of the Government of Canada.

Front cover and pages 2–3 photo credits: Sleeping Giant Provincial Park © Ontario Parks
Page 1 photo credits, clockwise from top left: © Hockey Hall of Fame; © Brian Lasenby/Shutterstock.com; © Collingwood Elvis Festival, Elvis Presley Enterprises and Dave West Photography; © Darlene Munro/Shutterstock.com; © Municipality of Chatham–Kent; © Ontario Parks; © Pictureguy/Shutterstock.com; © Joe Gilker/Dark Arts Astrophotography
Back cover photo credits, clockwise from top: © Kiev.Victor/Shutterstock.com; © Helen Filatova/Shutterstock.com; © Ontario Parks; © Elena Elisseeva/Shutterstock.com; © Tony Moran/Shutterstock.com

100 DESTINATIONS

Oxford County Cheese Trail

St. George's Anglican Church, Guelph

Elora Quarry, Elora

Chinatown, Toronto

Preface		9
SOUTHWESTERN ONTARIO		10
1	Basilica of Our Lady Immaculate & St. George's Anglican Church ⏐ Guelph	12
2	Blue Mountain Resort & Collingwood Elvis Festival ⏐ Collingwood	14
3	The Bruce Trail ⏐ Queenston–Tobermory	16
4	"Canada's Prettiest Town" & Its Historic Gaol ⏐ Goderich	18
5	"Classic Car Capital of Canada" ⏐ Chatham, Blenheim, Mitchell's Bay, Bothwell & Wallaceburg in Chatham–Kent	20
6	Fergus Scottish Festival & Highland Games ⏐ Fergus	22
7	Grand Bend Beach vs. Pinery Provincial Park ⏐ Lake Huron	24
8	Hillside Festival ⏐ Guelph	28
9	Long Point World Biosphere Reserve, Wildlife Area & Bird Observatory ⏐ Long Point	30
10	Mennonite Country ⏐ St. Jacobs	32
11	Museums of London ⏐ London	34
12	Oktoberfest ⏐ Kitchener–Waterloo	36
13	"Ontario's Most Beautiful Village" ⏐ Elora	38
14	Oxford County Cheese Trail ⏐ Ingersoll, Woodstock & Bright	42
15	Point Pelee National Park ⏐ Leamington	44
16	Riverfront Trail & Sculpture Park ⏐ Windsor	48
17	Salmon Tour & Tom Thomson Art Gallery ⏐ Owen Sound	50
18	Six Nations of the Grand River ⏐ Ohsweken	52
19	The Stratford Festival ⏐ Stratford	54
CENTRAL ONTARIO		56
TORONTO		
20	Aga Khan Museum & Ismaili Centre ⏐ North York	58
21	Art Gallery of Ontario ⏐ Toronto	60
22	BAPS Shri Swaminarayan Mandir ⏐ Etobicoke	62
23	Bata Shoe Museum ⏐ Toronto	64
24	Canadian National Exhibition & Royal Agricultural Winter Fair ⏐ Toronto	66
25	Casa Loma & Spadina Museum ⏐ Toronto	70
26	Chinatown ⏐ Toronto	72
27	CN Tower ⏐ Toronto	74
28	The Distillery Historic District ⏐ Toronto	76
29	High Park ⏐ Toronto	78
30	Hockey Hall of Fame ⏐ Toronto	80
31	Massey Hall & Roy Thomson Hall ⏐ Toronto	82

Roy Thompson Hall, Toronto

Webster Falls, Hamilton

Niagara Wine Country

Mazinaw Rock, Bon Echo

32	Royal Ontario Museum ǀ Toronto	86
33	St. Lawrence Market ǀ Toronto	90
34	Toronto Caribbean Carnival Parade ǀ Toronto	92
35	Toronto Pride Festival & Parade ǀ Toronto	94
36	The Word On The Street ǀ Toronto	96
37	Ball's Falls & Cataract Trail ǀ Jordan/Ball's Falls	98
38	Brock's Monument & Historic Fort George ǀ Queenston Heights	100
39	Canada's Largest Ribfest vs. North America's Largest Vegetarian Food Festival ǀ Burlington/Toronto	102
40	Canada's Wonderland ǀ Vaughan	104
41	Canadian Warplane Heritage Museum ǀ Hamilton/Mount Hope	106
42	City of Waterfalls ǀ Hamilton	108
43	Cobourg Beach & Sandcastle Festival ǀ Cobourg	112
44	Halton County Radial Railway Museum ǀ Milton	114
45	Halton High Points ǀ Mount Nemo, Rattlesnake Point, Kelso, Crawford Lake & Hilton Falls	116
46	Hiking Headwaters Country ǀ Erin, Caledon & Dufferin County	118
47	McMichael Canadian Art Collection ǀ Kleinburg	122
48	Niagara-on-the-Lake Historic District & the Shaw Festival ǀ Niagara-on-the-Lake	124
49	Niagara Falls ǀ Niagara Falls	126
50	Niagara Wine Country & Wine Festivals ǀ Niagara Peninsula	128
51	"Ontario's Best-Preserved Main Street" ǀ Port Hope	130
52	Remembrance Park ǀ Georgetown/Halton Hills	132
53	Royal Botanical Gardens ǀ Burlington	134
54	Sound of Music Festival ǀ Burlington	136
	EASTERN ONTARIO	138
55	Bon Echo Provincial Park & Mazinaw Rock ǀ Near Kaladar	140
56	Bonnechere Caves & Fourth Chute Falls ǀ Eganville	144
57	Family Day on the Waterway ǀ Brockville	148
58	Fort Henry National Historic Site ǀ Kingston	150
59	Fort Wellington National Historic Site & Battle of the Windmill National Historic Site ǀ Prescott	152
60	Historic Perth ǀ Perth	154
61	Kingston City Hall ǀ Kingston	156
62	Marmora SnoFest & Sled-Dog Races ǀ Marmora	158
63	North Frontenac Dark Sky Preserve ǀ South of Plevna	160
64	Pembroke's Heritage Murals ǀ Pembroke	162
65	Sandbanks Provincial Park ǀ Prince Edward County	164
66	The County ǀ Prince Edward County	166
67	Thousand Islands National Park ǀ St. Lawrence River	168
68	Upper Canada Village ǀ Morrisburg	170

OTTAWA

69	ByWard Market Ottawa	172
70	Canada Day on Parliament Hill Ottawa	174
71	Canadian Museum of Nature Ottawa	176
72	Canadian Tulip Festival Ottawa	178
73	Rideau Canal National Historic Site Ottawa–Kingston	182
74	Winterlude Ottawa	186

Rideau Canal, Ottawa

		188

COTTAGE COUNTRY

75	Agawa Canyon Train Tour Sault Ste. Marie	190
76	Algonquin Provincial Park & Barron Canyon Algonquin Provincial Park	192
77	Beausoleil Island Port Severn	196
78	Big Nickel, Dynamic Earth & Science North Sudbury	198
79	Canadian Canoe Museum Peterborough	200
80	Cross-Country Skiing in Muskoka Muskoka	202
81	Fathom Five National Marine Park & Flowerpot Island Tobermory	206
82	French River Provincial Park Alban	210
83	Haliburton Sculpture Forest Haliburton	214
84	Ice Fishing on Lake Simcoe Lake Simcoe	216
85	Killarney Provincial Park & the La Cloche Mountains Killarney	218
86	Manitoulin Island Indigenous Adventures Manitoulin Island	220
87	Mariposa Folk Festival Orillia	222
88	"Mineral Capital of Canada" Bancroft	224
89	Moose Safaris & Wolf Howls Algonquin Park	226
90	Muskoka Steamships & Discovery Centre Gravenhurst	228
91	Paddlepalooza Kayak Festival Parry Sound	230
92	Petroglyphs Provincial Park & National Historic Site Woodview/Peterborough	232
93	Sainte-Marie Among the Hurons National Historic Site Midland	234
94	Trent–Severn Waterway & Peterborough Lift Lock National Historic Site	
	Trenton–Peterborough–Port Severn	236
95	Wasaga Beach Provincial Park Wasaga Beach	238

Canadian Tulip Festival, Ottawa

Mariposa Festival, Orillia

NORTHERN ONTARIO

96	Kakabeka Falls Kakabeka Falls	240
97	Polar Bear Provincial Park Hudson Bay	244
98	Sleeping Giant Provincial Park & Ouimet Canyon Pass Lake	246
99	Terry Fox Memorial & Lookout Thunder Bay	248
100	Wabakimi Provincial Park Armstrong Station	250

	Acknowledgements	252
	References	253
	Photo Credits	254
	Index of Destinations	256

French River Provincial Park

Agawa Canyon, Sault Ste. Marie

PREFACE

Ontario is vast — 107,639,388 hectares (415,598 sq mi) of mostly wilderness and water — but its southern reaches are known for its many vibrant growing cities, the countless historic towns and villages along its highways and back roads. Ontario is also, of course, home to the nation's capital. There are far more than 100 remarkable things to see and do in a province this size, but the 100 destinations in *Unforgettable Ontario* are worthy and diverse places to start your adventures.

Included are the world's longest freshwater beach, longest barrier dune formation, largest tulip festival, largest collection of Canadian art, largest collection of hockey memorabilia and the western hemisphere's tallest free-standing structure. You will also find North America's largest cultural festival, most powerful waterfall, oldest three-day Scottish festival, its only ice dragon boat festival and its largest classical repertory theatre company, as well as Canada's largest annual book and magazine festival, largest free music festival, largest annual fair, largest ribfest, largest amusement and water park, largest museum, largest botanical gardens and its oldest and longest marked trail. There are UNESCO World Heritage Sites and World Biosphere Reserves, National Historic Sites and Dark Sky Preserves, national and provincial parks, cliffs, caves, waterfalls, cultural celebrations, art galleries and sculpture parks, theatrical and musical performance venues, notable works of architecture and Ontario's "Best-Preserved Main Street."

The 100 destinations appear in alphabetical order within four designated regions. These loosely mapped regions are not based on specific regional divisions or provincial tourism guidelines but were devised to suit the purposes of this book. In choice of destinations, there was also an emphasis on accessibility: Most of the locations and events can be reached within minutes to a few hours from anywhere in the province except its northern reaches.

Most of the information in this book was checked and double-checked against primary website references as well as relevant provincial, regional and/or municipal tourism sources, national and provincial parks services websites, and so on. However, if a loop trail is half a kilometre (0.3 mi) longer than your Fitbit states, your Fitbit may be correct. This is a book of proposed day trips and adventures — a celebration of Ontario — not a reference book.

As you enter these pages, I hope you will be as inspired as I am by Ontario's natural wonders and unparalleled scenery, its magnificent parks and nature reserves, its historic structures and charming villages, its art and architecture, its colourful festivals and diverse events and activities. I hope you like where this book takes you.

FACING PAGE: Looking across the lighted cascade of Horseshoe Falls to the city of Niagara Falls, Ontario.

SOUTHWESTERN
ONTARIO

1 ⁓ Basilica of Our Lady Immaculate & St. George's Anglican Church | Guelph

2 ⁓ Blue Mountain Resort & Collingwood Elvis Festival | Collingwood

3 ⁓ The Bruce Trail | Queenston–Tobermory

4 ⁓ "Canada's Prettiest Town" & Its Historic Gaol | Goderich

5 ⁓ "Classic Car Capital of Canada" | Chatham, Blenheim, Mitchell's Bay, Bothwell
   & Wallaceburg in Chatham–Kent

6 ⁓ Fergus Scottish Festival & Highland Games | Fergus

7 ⁓ Grand Bend Beach vs. Pinery Provincial Park | Lake Huron

8 ⁓ Hillside Festival | Guelph

9 ⁓ Long Point World Biosphere Reserve, Wildlife Area & Bird Observatory | Long Point

10 ⁓ Mennonite Country | St. Jacobs

11 ⁓ Museums of London | London

12 ⁓ Oktoberfest | Kitchener–Waterloo

13 ⁓ "Ontario's Most Beautiful Village" | Elora

14 ⁓ Oxford County Cheese Trail | Ingersoll, Woodstock & Bright

15 ⁓ Point Pelee National Park | Leamington

16 ⁓ Riverfront Trail & Sculpture Park | Windsor

17 ⁓ Salmon Tour & Tom Thomson Art Gallery | Owen Sound

18 ⁓ Six Nations of the Grand River | Ohsweken

19 ⁓ The Stratford Festival | Stratford

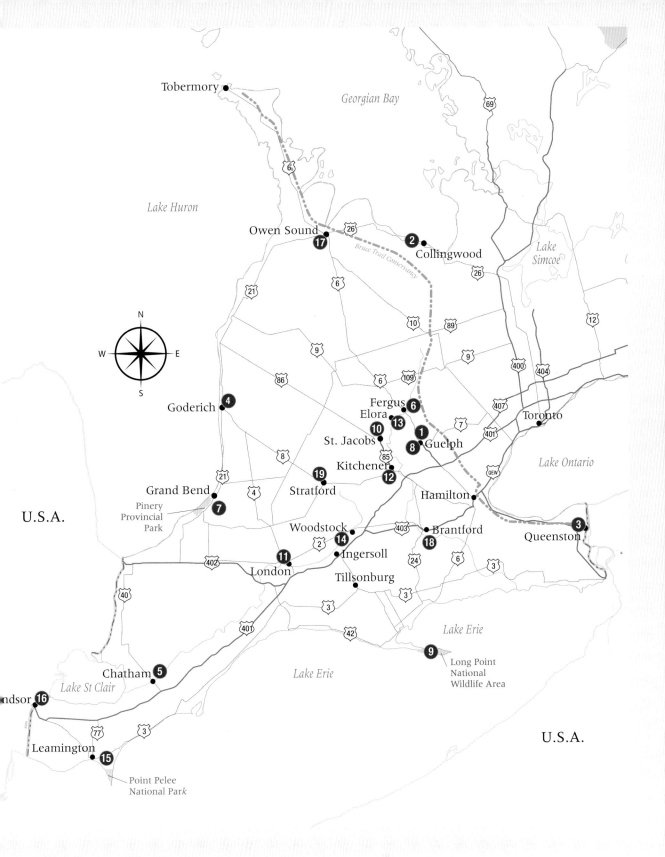

Tobermory

Georgian Bay

Lake Huron

Owen Sound **17** (26)

Bruce Trail Conservancy

2 Collingwood

(26)

Lake Simcoe

(69)

(12)

(21)

(6)

(10) (89)

(9)

(86)

(9) (9)

(400) (404)

Goderich **4**

(8)

(6) (109)

Fergus **6**

Elora **13**

St. Jacobs **10**

(85)

Kitchener

12

1

8 Guelph

(7)

(407)

(401)

Toronto

Lake Ontario

Grand Bend

Pinery Provincial Park

7

(21)

(4)

19

Stratford

Woodstock

Hamilton

QEW

(403) Brantford

3 Queenston

U.S.A.

(2)

14 Ingersoll

18

(24)

(6)

(3)

(402)

11 London

Tillsonburg

(3)

(3)

(40)

(401)

(3)

(42)

Lake Erie

9

Long Point National Wildlife Area

Chatham **5**

Lake Erie

Lake St Clair

ndsor **16**

(77) (3)

Leamington **15**

Point Pelee National Park

U.S.A.

11

1

BASILICA OF OUR LADY IMMACULATE & ST. GEORGE'S ANGLICAN CHURCH

~ Guelph

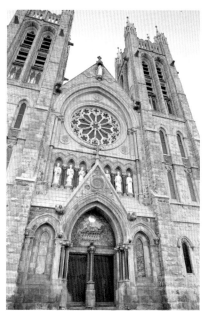

ABOVE LEFT: The magnificent Basilica of Our Lady Immaculate sits atop "Catholic Hill," visible from most neighbourhoods in Guelph. ABOVE RIGHT: The main entrance to the basilica and its two front-facing main towers.

Guelph is known for its beautiful churches, but best known and most prominently located is the Basilica of Our Lady Immaculate (formerly Church of Our Lady). Situated on the brow of a hill at the centre of old Guelph, its twin towers — said to have been inspired by medieval French cathedrals — can be seen from most parts of the city. In fact, city bylaws prohibit construction that may obscure sightlines, and no new building may rise taller than Our Lady.

The church was designed by Irish-Canadian architect Joseph Connolly, the principal architect for the Roman Catholic Church in Ontario at the time, and is considered by many to be his masterpiece. (Connolly's work includes St. Mary's Church in Toronto and St. Peter's Cathedral Basilica in London.)

Construction began in 1877, and the towers were completed in 1926. It is one of the most exceptional examples of the High Victorian Gothic Revival-style architecture to be found in Canada and was designated a National Historic Site

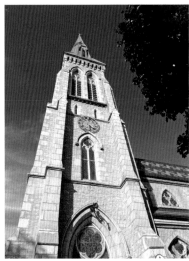

LEFT: Side view of St. George's Anglican Church, designed by Henry Langley in the English Gothic Revival tradition. ABOVE: St. George's steeple houses the 36 bells of the church's three-octave carillon.

Things to See & Do

- Attend a mass at the Basilica of Our Lady Immaculate.
- Take part in an architectural tour.
- Hear the choir and Casavant organ at St. George's.
- Attend a chamber or jazz performance.

Basilica of Our Lady
   Immaculate
28 Norfolk Street
Guelph, ON N1H 4H8
519-824-3951
churchofourlady.com

St. George's Anglican
   Church
99 Woolwich Street
Guelph, ON N1H 3V1
519-822-1366
saintgeorge.ca

in 1990. The designation notes: "… architectural details inspired by the French Gothic Revival, including a cruciform plan with side aisles, prominent nave, triforium arcades, apse with radiating chapels and ambulatory, twin-towered façade, spire at the central groin vault, and large rose windows; the sense of verticality, created by the use of steeply pitched roofs with gables, dormers, pinnacles, pointed arches, and tall narrow window openings; the symmetrically organized façade with its twin square towers with pinnacles and paired openings, massive rose window with bar tracery set in a moulded pointed arch, row of lintel statuary set within a blind arcade, and carved tympanum…." It also praises the interior craftsmanship — wood and stone carving, stained glass, ironwork, stencilling and mosaics. In 2014, Pope Francis designated the church a basilica.

Just a few blocks away stands stately St. George's Anglican Church. The current church replaced two earlier versions, which were located in nearby St. George's Square. Construction began in 1870 and was completed in 1873. It was designed by Henry Langley, the architect of many Ontario churches, including three others in Guelph. St. George's is a revival of the English Gothic medieval parish church, with different rooflines indicating the areas for nave, choir and sanctuary.

St. George's Anglican Church counts hundreds of Guelph families in its congregation, but it is also a popular site for community and cultural events — particularly musical ones. The church is home to a magnificent historic Casavant organ and a rare three-octave carillon and is renowned for its choirs. It hosts a three-season series of chamber music concerts, while opening its doors to avant-garde jazz performances during the Guelph Jazz Festival.

2

BLUE MOUNTAIN RESORT & COLLINGWOOD ELVIS FESTIVAL

～ Collingwood

Blue Mountain is a four-season recreational resort found on a section of the Niagara Escarpment just northwest of Collingwood. With a peak elevation of 220 metres (720 ft), it may be a stretch to call this piece of land a "mountain," but it has its thrills, and Ontario skiers have made its alpine operations the third busiest in Canada, after British Columbia's Whistler–Blackcomb and Quebec's Mont Tremblant. What Blue lacks in height, it makes up for in facilities and enthusiasm, offering a wide range of options for downhill, glade and Nordic (cross-country) skiing, as well as snowboarding.

Its 147 hectares (364 acres) of skiable slopes feature three freestyle terrain parks and 42 runs, including 30 lighted trails for night skiing. The longest run, Gord's Groove, lasts 1.6 kilometres (1 mile). Blue Mountain also boasts the largest beginner terrain in Ontario, making it family-friendly.

Blue's Ridge Runner Mountain Coaster operates year-round. Riders control

Blue Mountain Resort is Canada's third-busiest ski destination. It offers three freestyle terrain parks and 42 runs, including 30 lighted trails for night skiing.

TOP RIGHT: Collingwood hosts the "World's Largest Elvis Festival," with 18,000 annual visitors. BOTTOM RIGHT: Blue Mountain Village offers a variety of accommodations, activities, special events, festivals and more than 40 shops and restaurants.

their own speeds — up to 42 kilometres per hour (26 mph) — as they twist and turn through 1,085 metres (3,560 ft) of varied terrain. Winter activities also include backcountry snowshoeing, snow tubing and pond skating on the resort, with snowmobile tours, sleigh rides and winter caving available nearby.

Among summer's attractions are the Wind Rider Triple Zips, which send riders from platform to platform at a height of 15 metres (50 ft). The Apex Bagjump allows would-be stunt jumpers to fall freely from heights up to

6.5 metres (21 ft) onto an air bag waiting below. The Timber High Ropes course encourages individuals and teams to navigate the best route up ladders, across bridges and down zip lines. Woodlot Low Ropes — geared to younger climbers — involves ropes, logs, beams, cables and cargo nets. Problem-solvers gain greater confidence with each mastered challenge.

The resort's Plunge Aquatic Centre houses indoor and outdoor swimming pools, with waterslides and rope swings. Guests also have access to the popular climbing wall, an 18-hole par-67 putting course, an 18-hole golf course, indoor tennis courts, hiking trails, open-air gondola rides, mountaintop Segway tours, concerts and special events.

Speaking of special events, nearby Collingwood hosts "The World's Largest Elvis Festival," traditionally on the weekend before the Civic Holiday long weekend. The festival attracts 18,000 visitors annually.

Competitors from far and near perform for a panel of judges, with the top 26 competitors moving on to the semi-finals to perform two songs each. Each is judged on vocal skills, performance style, stage presence/showmanship, appearance and "overall Tribute to Elvis authenticity." There are categories for professional, nonprofessional and youth Elvises. The overall winner in the professional division travels to Memphis, Tennessee, as the Collingwood festival's representative in the Ultimate Elvis Tribute Artist Contest held annually in August.

Things to See & Do

- Ski Ontario's #1 resort.
- Ride the Ridge Runner Mountain Coaster.
- Navigate the Timber Challenge High Ropes Course.
- Attend The World's Largest Elvis Festival.

Blue Mountain
108 Jozo Weider Blvd.
Blue Mountains, ON
L9Y 3Z2
705-445-0231
1-877-445-0231
bluemountain.ca

Collingwood
 Elvis Festival
97 Hurontario Street
Collingwood, ON
L9Y 2L9
705-444-2500
 Ext. 3279
collingwoodelvis
 festival.com

3

THE BRUCE TRAIL
~ Queenston–Tobermory

Most of us have heard the saying, "Life is about the journey, not the destination." It's also a good way to look at the Bruce Trail. You could hike its entire length in about 30 days — if you're fit and willing to hike at least eight hours a day every day. Or you could spend years enjoying its many segments and links.

At 840 kilometres (522 mi) long and with over 440 kilometres (273 mi) of side trails, the Bruce Trail is the oldest and longest marked trail in Canada. Its southern terminus is along the Niagara River, marked by a cairn on park grounds east of Brock's Monument in Queenston. Its northern terminus is in Tobermory, at the tip of the Bruce Peninsula.

The Bruce Trail follows the edge of the Niagara Escarpment (a UNESCO World Biosphere Reserve) and winds through numerous well-known parks and conservation areas, including Woodend Conservation Area in Niagara-on-the-Lake, Battle-

BELOW: The Grotto, near Tobermory, is a unique natural shoreline cave that looks out upon the clear blue waters off the Bruce Peninsula. FACING PAGE: Wooden boardwalks appear frequently along the Bruce Trail, often protecting fragile plant species nearby.

field Park in Stoney Creek, Dundas Valley Conservation Area, Mount Nemo Conservation Area, Rattlesnake Point Conservation Area, Crawford Lake Conservation Area, Mono Cliffs Provincial Park and Bruce Peninsula National Park.

The Bruce Trail Conservancy's "Trails A–Z" lists more than 100 different trail segments with over 300 access points. The Conservancy's mandate is to conserve all the land that the trail crosses, and the organization works with the Government of Ontario, local municipalities, local conservation authorities and private landowners to this end.

Despite the fact that the Bruce Trail and the Niagara Escarpment run through some of the most populated regions of Ontario, wildlife biologists have stated that this may be the most biologically diverse region in the province. It is home to 53 species of mammals, 36 species of reptiles and amphibians, 90 species of fish and over 350 species of birds.

Many sections of the trail feature waterfalls where streams spill over the Escarpment. Each year, more than 400,000 people hike, cross-country ski or snowshoe the Bruce Trail, watching for wildlife and appreciating the scenery. There are numerous books to guide you, and the Bruce Trail Conservancy's website is excellent.

While it has been calculated that 7,000,000 people live within 100 kilometres (62 mi) of the trail, once you're on it, you'll feel like you've escaped the stress of urban life.

Things to See & Do

- Experience the hundreds of hiking options.
- Encounter Ontario's most diverse wildlife.
- Marvel at the Escarpment scenery.
- Snowshoe or cross-country ski in winter.

Bruce Trail Conservancy
55 Head Street, Unit 101
Dundas, ON L9H 3H8
905-529-6821
1-800-665- 4453
brucetrail.org
ontariotrails.on.ca

4

"CANADA'S PRETTIEST TOWN" & ITS HISTORIC GAOL

~ Goderich

Whether you are gazing west from the bluffs or the beach, Goderich's Lake Huron sunsets rank consistently among Ontario's best.

It has been claimed that it was Queen Elizabeth II who first called Goderich "the prettiest town in Canada," but if so, she must have formed her opinion from photographs, as no reigning monarch has ever visited this picturesque southwestern Ontario community. No matter. If not *the* prettiest, it is *one* of the prettiest. Situated at the mouth of the Maitland River, on the eastern shore of Lake Huron, Goderich is renowned for its beautiful sunsets. It also holds numerous Communities in Bloom awards, and its 19th-century architecture is well preserved.

The Port of Goderich is the county seat of Huron County, with a population of approximately 7,600. It was founded by John Galt and William "Tiger" Dunlop of the Canada Company in 1827 and named for Frederick John Robinson, 1st

ABOVE: Goderich's eight primary streets radiate out from an octagonal centre known as "The Square." RIGHT: The Huron County Museum's exhibits chronicle the town's development as a fishing village, busy port and railway hub.

Things to See & Do

- Walk the old town streets.
- Swim at Rotary Cove Beach.
- Visit Huron County Museum & Historic Gaol.
- Find out what's on at the Livery Theatre.

Huron County Museum & Historic Gaol
91 Hamilton Street
Goderich, ON
N7A 1R1
519-524-6600
1-800-280-7637
goderich.ca
huroncountymuseum. ca/gaol

Viscount Goderich, who was briefly the British prime minister that year. (He resigned after 144 days in office, no reflection on his namesake community.)

The town's two museums are worth a visit. The Marine Museum, open in July and August, focuses on the hardy souls who worked the port, pioneering fishing and shipping on Lake Huron. The Huron County Museum maintains the county's archives and houses gallery space for current exhibitions. Its permanent exhibits relate to the settlement and development of Huron County and feature a full-sized locomotive and an extensive collection of military memorabilia (including a Sherman tank). And don't miss the Huron County Gaol, a National Historic Site. This unique octagonal prison operated from 1841 until 1972. Visitors can explore the building's courtroom, holding cells, cell blocks, working rooms and living quarters. The gaol is the site of the last public hanging in Canada.

Another popular attraction is the historic Livery Theatre building, home to the Goderich Little Theatre company, the Livery Film Festival, live musical performances and numerous community arts events.

The Goderich waterfront has three public beaches connected by a boardwalk. At the north end is the main beach, where you can swim or sit and watch lake freighters being loaded with salt on the other side of the pier. St. Christopher's Beach is a bit farther south. And at the far end of the boardwalk is family-friendly Rotary Cove, with a sand beach and lifeguards.

5

"CLASSIC CAR CAPITAL OF CANADA"

~ Chatham, Blenheim, Mitchell's Bay, Bothwell & Wallaceburg in Chatham–Kent

BELOW, CLOCKWISE FROM TOP LEFT: The antique boats kick off the Wallaceburg Antique Motor & Boat Outing; the expanding display of vintage fire trucks is a highlight for young and old; a "Pinehurst Green" 1959 Cadillac at Chatham's Retrofest.

Chatham–Kent can trace its automotive roots back more than a century. From about 1905 to 1912, Chatham's Robert Gray built Ford bodies for the Walkerville (Windsor) factory, as well as bodies for the Chatham Motor Car Company (1906–1909). In 1915, Gray obtained Canadian rights from the Dort Motor Company, based in Flint, Michigan, to manufacture the Gray-Dort automobile. Over its 10-year lifespan, Gray-Dort built approximately 26,000 sedans, coupes and touring cars. A few communities in the regional municipality continue to produce auto parts.

And then there's RM Sotheby's (formerly RM Auctions and RE Restorations) — "world's largest vintage automobile auction house" and "world's largest vintage automobile restoration company" — with offices in the United States, United Kingdom and Germany, but whose headquarters is in Blenheim, Ontario. (Fancy a 1935 Duesenberg Model J Cabriolet for $2 million?) The designation "Classic Car Capital of Canada" comes from RM's position in the world of vintage automobiles, as well as the unusual abundance of classic car events in the region.

ABOVE LEFT: Answering the question: What's this beauty got under the hood? ABOVE RIGHT: Eye-catching flame work on a customized hot rod.

Things to See & Do

- Attend Chatham's Retrofest Classic Car Cruise.
- Check out the Antique Car, Truck, Tractor & Motorcycle Show at Mitchell's Marine Bay Park.
- Find vintage car parts for your car at the Bothwell Car Show's Car Corral & Automotive Flea Market.
- See WAMBO's 500 vintage cars, motorcycles, fire trucks, boats and airplanes.

Chatham–Kent Tourism
25 Creek Road
Chatham, ON
N7M 0L1
519-360-1998
1-800-561-6125
chatham-kent.ca/
tourism

Held on the last weekend in May, Chatham's Retrofest is a celebration of automotive (and other) nostalgia. More than 600 classic cars and trucks were on display at a recent street festival. Friday's marquee event is the Classic Car Cruise. Drivers begin at the John D. Bradley Convention Centre and make their way, in two waves, alongside the Thames River to the staging area on historic downtown King Street.

Although the RM Sotheby's classics remain under lock and key, the Blenheim Classics Auto Show & Cruise Night is a lively event held in late June. Cruise Night starts at Glad Tidings Church and makes its way along Erie Beach before returning to Blenheim. On Saturday, more than 150 vintage cars take their places of honour along downtown's Talbot Street West, and an estimated 3,500 area residents and visitors turn out to admire the year's crop. The show is for cars dating 1988 or earlier.

The Mitchell's Bay Antique Car, Truck, Tractor & Motorcycle Show is held in Mitchell's Marine Bay Park, on Lake St. Clair, in mid-July. The show is for pre-1997 vehicles. The turnout for the antique tractors is impressive.

The Bothwell Car Show, one of Canada's largest daylong shows with more than 1,200 vehicles and 250 venders, takes place in Victoria Park on the weekend following the August Civic Holiday weekend. The annual Car Corral & Automotive Flea Market opens at 8 a.m. on Friday. That evening, the Vintage Auto Parade gives everyone a peek at Saturday's standouts. An estimated 6,500 spectators gather to admire the gleaming vintage automobiles, pickups, panel vans, trucks, hot rods, customized vehicles and one-of-a-kind transportation creations.

Finally, the Wallaceburg Antique Motor & Boat Outing (WAMBO) bills itself as "Canada's largest and foremost antique transportation show." It takes place each August and features more than 500 vintage cars, motorcycles, fire trucks, boats and airplanes. Events include the Terry Glover Memorial Cruise, the Car & Motorcycle Show, the Fire Truck Show, the Antique & Custom Bicycle Show, the Annual Toy & Model Show, Soap Box Racing, the Police Boat Parade, Cardboard Boat Racing, the Fire Truck Parade, the awards ceremonies for car owners and live music.

6

FERGUS SCOTTISH FESTIVAL & HIGHLAND GAMES

~ Fergus

The Pipes & Drums Competition is a pride-stirring event for anyone with a tartan connection. Prizes are awarded to pipers and drummers at both professional and amateur levels.

Celebrating Scottish-Canadian culture for over 70 years, the annual Fergus Scottish Festival & Highland Games is the oldest three-day Scottish festival in North America. Townsman Alex Robertson founded it as a community-wide celebration of Scottish life and customs in 1946.

Held on the second full weekend in August, the festivities begin with the Pipes, Plaid and Pageantry Parade on Thursday evening in downtown Fergus. Friday night kicks off with "Tattoo'd in Tradition," with rousing performances by military-style pipe bands and marching ensembles. Recent festivals have welcomed more than 60 individual clan societies, with each society maintaining a Clan Cabana on Avenue of the Clans. Here, information is exchanged about specific clans, their role in Scottish history and the clan relationships that still

CLOCKWISE FROM ABOVE LEFT: A junior pipe major leads at the Pipes, Plaid and Pageantry Parade; the festival welcomes as many as 60 clan societies; steady concentration before tossing the caber; highland dancers engage in competition.

Things to See & Do

- Take part in the Pipes, Plaid and Pageantry Parade.
- Watch the kilted athletic competitions.
- Learn the intricacies of highland dance.
- Research your clan.

Fergus Scottish Festival
P.O. Box 25
Fergus, ON N1M 2W7
519-787-0099
1-866-871-9442
fergusscottishfestival.
com

exist in modern Scottish and North American culture. There is also a Heritage Tent, as well as lectures in the Genealogy Centre.

A popular draw for visitors is the World and National Scottish Heavy Events Competition. "The Heavies" features powerful kilted men participating in such challenges as the Caber Toss, the 16- and 22-pound Scottish Hammer Throw, the 22-pound Braemar Stone, the 56-pound Weight for Distance, and the 56-pound Weight for Height.

The Pipes & Drums Competition offers prizes for Professional Piper, Professional Drummer, Amateur Piper, Amateur Drummer and Under-19 Piper of the Day. Music continues with a Saturday-night Celtic Traditions concert.

Sanctioned by the Scottish Official Board of Highland Dancing, the Fergus Scottish Festival Championship was created in 2006 in celebration of the festival's 60th anniversary. Dancers perform the Highland Fling, the Sword Dance, the Seann Triubhas and the Strathspey & Half Tulloch, with champions for each dance and an overall champion.

The Fergus Highland Games 10k Run supports local youth athletic programs. Participants run through Fergus's charming neighbourhoods and the scenic adjacent countryside before returning to Victoria Park.

Many other Ontario communities hold summer festivals to celebrate their Scottish heritage, including the Glengarry Highland Games in Maxville, the North Lanark Highland Games in Almonte, the Kingston Scottish Festival, the Kincardine Scottish Festival & Highland Games and the Cobourg Scottish Festival & Highland Games.

GRAND BEND BEACH VS. PINERY PROVINCIAL PARK

～ Lake Huron

A re you an extrovert or an introvert? Do you like to join the fun or make your own? You can have it either way within a roughly 10-kilometre (6 mi) stretch of Lake Huron shoreline.

Grand Bend embraces its reputation as "Florida North" and "Ontario's West Coast." Weekend tourism grew in tandem with automobile ownership through the 1900s, and "The Bend," with its white sandy beaches, became a popular sum-

RIGHT: Pinery Provincial Park has nine day-use beaches, two of which are dog-friendly. BELOW: Night descends on the light at the end of the pier, Grand Bend Beach. *National Geographic* voted the area among the world's 10 best places to watch sunsets.

mer destination for young families. Today, the town's year-round population of 2,000 welcomes as many as 50,000 visitors on a holiday long weekend. Cottages and trailers are rented, hotels fill up, and vacation homes are bought and sold in adjacent communities such as Oakwood Park, Southcott Pines and Beach O'Pines.

The sun-and-surf crowd flock to the Main Beach by the thousands. Colourful umbrellas and towels create a festive patchwork. Swimmers swim. Parasailors parasail. Tanned bodies grasp for volleyballs, footballs and Frisbees. The North Beach tends to be occupied by young sun worshippers, and the mood is marginally calmer. The South Beach is typically the realm of intergenerational families, everyone minding the children and grandchildren as they dash in and out of the warm, shallow water.

In the daytime, Grand Bend's Main Street offers essential businesses, unique boutiques and small art galleries. At night, the many bars and restaurants come to life. The Huron Country Playhouse, at the edge of town, presents full-scale productions in two auditoriums throughout the summer.

Southeast of town, Grand Bend Motorplex has a drag strip and multiple courses for karts, cars and motorcycles. The Motorplex hosts an International Hot Rod Association race and the IHRA Canadian Nationals, Canada's largest and longest-running drag race.

For a quieter experience featuring the same scenery and the same spectacular sunsets, simply go seven kilometres (4.4 mi) south to Pinery Provincial Park. The Pinery shares the same beach-and-dune landscape as Grand Bend, but it is a natural-environment-class provincial park created to preserve the oak savannah and the coastal dune ecosystem.

The park is popular, so you will encounter other visitors and campers, but the 1,275 campsites are spread over 2,532 hectares (6,257 acres).

Pinery Provincial Park features 10 walking trails and a 14-kilometre (9 mi) bike trail. You can also rent all manner of self-propelled watercraft — canoe, paddleboat, single or double kayak, even hydro bike — and explore the Old Ausable Channel, a provincially significant wetland. ﹌

Things to See & Do

- Join the sun-and-fun crew on Grand Bend's Main Beach.
- Enjoy a musical at the Huron Country Playhouse.
- Catch a sunset among the dunes in Pinery Provincial Park.
- Explore the Old Ausable Channel via canoe or kayak.

Grand Bend Tourism
1-888-338-2001
grandbendtourism.com

Pinery Provincial Park
9526 Lakeshore Road
 RR2
Grand Bend, ON
N0M 1T0
519-243-2220
ontarioparks.com/park/
 pinery

TOP: The park's coastal dune ecosystem supports extraordinary biodiversity. ABOVE: Pinery Provincial Park's rare and fragile oak savannah. FACING PAGE: A boardwalk protects plants and dunes in Pinery Provincial Park.

8

HILLSIDE FESTIVAL
∼ Guelph

Most music festivals are about the musical guests — *Look who's performing this year!* Hillside Festival is all about the vibe. It has been said that Guelph is second only to British Columbia's Salt Spring Island in resident number of groovy tie-dye-wearing granola connoisseurs, musicians, artisans and activists. It's a source of community pride.

Check out Hillside's vision statement: "Hillside will create a more vibrant and caring world by promoting altruism, equality, environmentalism and peacemaking in every aspect of its work." Good vibes. And the festival's organizers and volunteers work hard to fulfill every word of that statement.

That doesn't mean music takes a back seat. Recent marquee performers have included Broken Social Scene, City and Colour, Arcade Fire, k-os, Stars, Cowboy Junkies, Metric, Feist, Yukon Blonde, The Arkells, Sarah Harmer, Tokyo Police Club, Bombay Bicycle Club, Sloan and The Weakerthans. The music is carefully

FACING PAGE: The Bahamas Junkanoo Legends parade around the festival site. LEFT: Alyssa Delbaere-Sawchuk of the New Canadian Global Music Orchestra performs on the Main Stage in 2017. BELOW: The audience is seized by the dancing spirit at a Lake Stage performance.

curated, and the festival's four stages offer a steady stream of thoughtfully selected eclectic, mostly independent, mostly Canadian talent performing everything from folk to funk, hip-hop to roots rock, urban to outlaw and electronic to spoken word. Hillside is not a rock festival. It is not a folk festival. It is a music festival — but it is also a people festival.

On Saturday and Sunday, there are dozens of workshops conducted at various locations. You can learn the basics of singing, songwriting, salsa dancing, salsa making, micro-farming, rain gardening, silk screening, kundalini yoga, acrobatic yoga, Thai yoga massage, kung fu, conflict mediation, Kirtan meditation, "The Fine Art of Giving Great Hugs," and much more. Meanwhile, the Rainbow Stage area features music, readings and activities for children.

More than two dozen unique craft vendors display their wares at the Artisan Market, while food vendors cater to a wide variety of tastes and appetites and offer vegetarian, vegan, organic, gluten-free and fair-trade options.

Hillside Festival received the 2016 award for Best Green Operations Festival from Canadian Music Week as well as the Festival and Events Ontario award for Best Greening of a Festival over eight consecutive years. Vendors serve food on reusable plates, cups and cutlery, all of which are collected and washed by volunteer "Dish Ninjas." A City of Guelph water tanker provides Guelph tap water free of charge to festival goers with reusable containers. At Hillside, throwaway plastic bottles are strictly taboo.

Go for the music. Stay for the smiling, happy people.

Things to See & Do

- Discover a new favourite band.
- Take part in a drum circle.
- Attend inspiring workshops.
- Talk to strangers.

Hillside Festival
341 Woolwich Street
Guelph, ON N1H 3W4
519-763-6396
hillsidefestival.ca

9

LONG POINT WORLD BIOSPHERE RESERVE, WILDLIFE AREA & BIRD OBSERVATORY

~ Long Point

Reaching almost 40 kilometres (25 mi) into Lake Erie, Long Point is the world's longest freshwater sand spit. Through the ongoing support of conservation groups and all levels of government, it continues to exist as a natural oasis, despite being only a stone's throw from Canada's most densely populated region.

This sandy spit is a UNESCO World Biosphere Reserve and home to Long Point Provincial Park, Long Point National Wildlife Area and the Long Point Bird Observatory/Bird Studies Canada, North America's oldest bird observatory.

The Long Point National Wildlife Area makes up the core of the biosphere reserve. Some 370 species of birds, 102 species of fish, 46 species of mammals, 34 species of amphibians and reptiles and 91 species of butterflies have been recorded here. Habitats include woodlands, sand dunes, bluffs, marshes, ponds, meadows, beaches and lakeshore.

ABOVE: A rough-legged hawk in flight. RIGHT: Children run along a stretch of fine sand beach at Long Point Provincial Park.

ABOVE, LEFT AND RIGHT: Long Point's vital marshlands.; the barn swallow, one of Long Point's 370 recorded species.

Things to See & Do

- Go for the birds — some 370 species.
- Count the countless species of amphibians, reptiles and mammals.
- See the monarch butterflies in August and September.
- Dive among the 200 ships in the "Long Point Triangle."

Long Point
  Provincial Park
P.O. Box 99
350 Erie Blvd
Port Rowan, ON
N0E 1M0
519-586-2133
ontarioparks.com/park/
  longpoint
birdscanada.org/
  longpoint/

The spit contains some of Canada's largest tracts of temperate Carolinian forest and is home to 1,384 species of plants. Hardwood species, including the sugar maple, American beech, basswood, red ash, white oak and butternut dominate, but you will also find the sweet gum, tulip tree, cucumber tree, American sycamore, pawpaw, Kentucky coffee-tree, honey locust, black tupelo, blue ash, sassafras, pignut hickory, shellbark hickory, black oak, pumpkin ash, Ohio buckeye, pin oak, black walnut and red mulberry.

Long Point's marsh areas are main stopover points for migrating land birds and waterfowl. The Long Point Bird Observatory was established in 1960 to monitor migrant birds on the point, and the national headquarters of Bird Studies Canada overlooks Long Point's Inner Bay. The downloadable "Long Point Birding Trail," from Bird Studies Canada, provides an overview of local birding hot spots and has been designed to maximize the chances of seeing a good selection of birds. All of the Birding Trail's 40 sites are publicly accessible. Waterfowl viewing is at its best in March and April, migrating birds in fall and spring, and monarch butterflies (on their way to Mexico) in August and September.

Ship travel across the Great Lakes reached an all-time high in the mid- to late 1800s. Long Point was a navigational landmark — and hazard — for ships travelling across Lake Erie. Constantly shifting sandbars often caught ships off guard, and Long Point Peninsula has claimed more the 200 vessels — more than the Bermuda Triangle. As a result, Long Point has also become a top destination for Great Lakes diving enthusiasts.

10

MENNONITE COUNTRY
∿ St. Jacobs

The West Montrose Covered Bridge is the oldest of its kind in Canada. Completed in 1881, it is still used by pedestrians, Mennonite buggies and light local traffic.

As you venture north of Waterloo, in Woolwich Township, the roads straighten and large barns and farmhouses rise from well-tended fields. Just minutes beyond the modern bustle of Kitchener–Waterloo, you enter a different world. When you begin to pass the plainly clad Old Order Mennonites travelling in their horse-drawn buggies along the shoulders of the roads, it feels as if you've been transported back in time.

In the early 1800s, Mennonites from Pennsylvania bought a large tract of land in the township and moved north. As the 19th century progressed, some of these new settlers, known as the "Old Order," elected to eschew new inventions and technologies, believing these would erode their values of humility and simple living. The area around St Jacobs is home to the largest population of Old Order Mennonites in Canada, and it is not uncommon to see a farmer

LEFT: The St. Jacobs Farmers' Market main building and outdoor displays. BELOW: A group of young Mennonite women meet at the market.

Things to See & Do

- Visit Canada's largest year-round farmers' market.
- Learn about Mennonite culture at the Mennonite Story Visitor Centre.
- Peruse the wares of St. Jacobs' many talented artisans.
- Pay the toll at the "Kissing Bridge."

St. Jacobs Country
P.O. Box 310
1386 King Street North
St. Jacobs, ON
N0B 2N0
519-664-2293 Ext. 212
1-800-265-3353
stjacobs.com

ploughing his fields with a five-horse hitch, an entire community working together to erect a barn with simple hand tools in just two or three days, and boys of all ages playing post-chores baseball in dark pants, white shirts and suspenders.

That said, there are many different Mennonite groups. Some more progressive Mennonites have adopted much of mainstream culture. Still others have been selective regarding the technology they use. The Mennonite Story Visitor Centre, on the main street of St. Jacobs, is a great place to learn about the history, culture and faith of Mennonite people in this region of Ontario.

St. Jacobs features dozens of artisan businesses in historic buildings, including the Country Mill, the Village Silos, the Mill Shed and the Old Factory. Visitors can watch artisans make pottery, quilts, jewellery, glass vases, stained-glass doors, miniature dollhouses and more. The village also has two blacksmith shops.

Three kilometres (1.9 mi) south of the village centre is the St. Jacobs Farmers' Market. This combination farmers' market and flea market is said to be the largest year-round farmers' market in Canada and attracts about a million visitors annually.

While you're in the area, be sure to visit the West Montrose Covered Bridge. This local landmark is the last surviving wooden covered bridge in Ontario, and the oldest such bridge in Canada. It was built in 1880–1881 by barn-builder brothers John and Benjamin Bear and can still be used by pedestrians, buggy traffic and vehicles that weigh less than three tons. It is also known as the "Kissing Bridge." Local girls were warned to be wary when the horse pulling their escort's buggy stopped inside the bridge, as a kiss might be demanded as a toll to cross it.

11

MUSEUMS OF LONDON
~ London

BELOW TOP: Eldon House, London's oldest residence, maintains its 19th-century appearance. BELOW BOTTOM: The London Children's Museum is a distinctly hands-on learning environment.

For its size, this southwestern Ontario city has more than its fair share of museums, which makes it a perfect day-trip destination, whether your interests lean toward archaeology, medicine, military history or jet aircraft.

The Museum of Ontario Archaeology, at 1600 Attawandaron Road, is devoted to the study, display and interpretation of the human occupation of southwestern Ontario over the past 13,000 years. The museum is located adjacent to the Lawson Prehistoric Village, an archaeological site dating to the 16th century.

Located at 421 Ridout Street North, in downtown London, Museum London's collection holds more than 45,000 regional artifacts, which tell the fascinating story of London's history and the individual accomplishments of its many noteworthy citizens. The museum's art collection features more than 5,000 works by regional and national artists.

One of London's most famous residents was Sir Frederick Grant Banting (1891–1941). Banting House National Historic Site, at 442 Adelaide Street North, celebrates Dr. Banting's life and career, including his co-discovery of insulin, one of the most important advancements in 20th-century medicine. Permanent exhibitions also consider Banting the artist and war hero, as well as the Flame of Hope campaign.

Eldon House, at 481 Ridout Street North, is London's oldest residence, home to four generations of the Harris family, and its architecture is an excellent example of Georgian and Regency styles. Since 1960, when it was donated to the City of London, it has been maintained in its 19th-century appearance, with Harris family heirlooms, furnishings and keepsakes on public display.

The Royal Canadian Regiment Museum is located at Wolseley Barracks, 701 Oxford Street East. It is dedicated to chronicling the Royal Canadian Regiment. The museum collection includes a vast and ever-expanding variety of artifacts, including a wooden cross

CLOCKWISE FROM ABOVE LEFT: Guards in period costume at Wolseley Barracks; Museum London holds an excellent art collection; the Jet Aircraft Museum celebrates the modern RCAF by preserving aircraft like the JAM T-33.

Things to See & Do

- Visit the 500-year-old Lawson Prehistoric Village.
- Learn the story of insulin at Banting House.
- Take a house tour of London's oldest residence.
- Spend an afternoon at Wolseley Barracks.

London Information Centres
696 Wellington Road South or
391 Wellington Street
London, ON
519-661-5000
1-800-265-2602
londontourism.ca

from Flanders Field, regimental memorials, medals, uniforms, weapons, military equipment and vehicles, period artwork, archival documents and even musical instruments.

The Secrets of Radar Museum, at 2155-B Crumlin Side Road, preserves the experiences, stories and history of the nearly 6,000 Canadian remarkable men and women who helped develop, operate, maintain and defend Canadian radar, both at home and abroad.

The Jet Aircraft Museum, located at the London International Airport, celebrates the modern Royal Canadian Air Force and the valiant Canadian men and women who flew these aircraft during times of war, peace and peacekeeping. The museum strives to keep representative historic aircraft in the air and ready to appear at major aviation events.

Finally, the London Children's Museum, at 21 Wharncliffe Road South, provides a distinctly child-centred, hands-on environment for learning. Exhibits and stimulating activities allow them to explore history and heritage, investigate the complexities of social relationships and science, and celebrate the beauty in art and culture.

12

OKTOBERFEST
～ Kitchener–Waterloo

Based on the original German celebration, Kitchener–Waterloo's Oktoberfest bills itself as the second-largest Bavarian festival in North America and the second-largest Oktoberfest in the world. The nine-day festival is held each October, beginning on the Friday before Canadian Thanksgiving and continuing until the following Saturday. You might set aside Sunday for your recovery, as the festival's most popular attractions tend to involve beer.

Oktoberfest attracts as many as 700,000 visitors annually. Thousands celebrate in the nearly 20 Festhallen — licensed Bavarian-decorated buildings and tents with capacities ranging from 250 to 3,400 people. Each Festhallen offers German folk-music (oompah) bands, Bavarian dancers and traditional German cuisine. Other musical opportunities include Rocktoberfest — concert events featuring rock bands — as well as traditional polka.

The twin cities of Kitchener–Waterloo, as well as surrounding Waterloo County, have a long history of German traditions, a result of the Mennonite immigration from Pennsylvania and the arrival of immigrants directly from Germany in the mid-19th century. Many German-Canadians reside here today, and it is not unusual to hear German spoken on the street and in area shops.

The hub of Kitchener–Waterloo's Oktoberfest is the Willkommen Platz (Welcome Centre) in Kitchener City Hall's downtown Carl Zehr Square. The Platz is open every day during the festival, and its "Bavarian Village" features daily entertainment and activities, as well as official souvenirs and visitor information.

Of course, an official keg-tapping starts the festival, and that ritual is fol-

BELOW, LEFT TO RIGHT: During Oktoberfest, everyone is German. Celebrations include Festhallen gatherings; the Miss Oktoberfest pageant; encounters with mascots Onkel Hans and Tante Frieda; and plenty of traditional food, music and dance. FACING PAGE, TOP: Beer fuels the ceremonies, with roughly 40 official keg-tapping events.

Things to See & Do

- Catch the German-culture-themed Thanksgiving Day parade.
- Enjoy drink and dance at the Festhallen.
- Visit the Bavarian Village at Willkommen Platz.
- Experience German-Canadian hospitality.

Kitchener–Waterloo Oktoberfest
17 Benton Street
Kitchener, ON
N2G 3G9
519-570-4267
1-888-294-4267
oktoberfest.ca

lowed by more than 40 family and cultural events, including craft shows, barrel races, a car show, dance competitions, a fashion show, cooking demonstrations, axe-throwing, arm-wrestling, hockey and slo-pitch softball tournaments and a cycling race. Also, beer.

An Oktoberfest five-kilometre Fun Run precedes the annual Thanksgiving Day parade. Attended by an estimated 150,000 people, Kitchener–Waterloo's Thanksgiving Day parade is one of the biggest in Canada and is televised nation-wide on CTV.

You often hear the German term *Gemütlichkeit* associated with these festivities. Roughly translated, it means "warm friendliness." At Oktoberfest, everyone is German.

13

"ONTARIO'S MOST BEAUTIFUL VILLAGE"

∽ Elora

In a province bursting at the seams with well-maintained historic towns and charming riverside villages, Elora still stands out for its architecture, natural beauty and lively arts community.

Many of Elora's early settlers were Scottish pioneers who left their mark in the community's finely crafted limestone and double-brick houses. Its numerous small specialty shops, boutiques, pubs, cafés, restaurants and art galleries are often housed in immaculate 19th-century limestone architecture.

The well-known Elora Mill, built in 1836, has been partially destroyed on several occasions but always returns tastefully restored. Its view of the Elora Gorge Falls, with "The Tooth of Time" island at midstream, is mesmerizing.

The backs of Mill Street's shops and cafés reflected in the lazy Grand River.

Surrounded by high, sheer limestone cliffs, the Elora Quarry is one of the region's most popular swimming holes.

Things to See & Do

- Explore the cliffs and caves of the Gorge.
- Attend performances at the Elora Festival or Riverfest Elora.
- Catch an indie film at the historic Gorge Cinema.
- Shop the boutiques and specialty stores at village centre.

Elora Information Centre
9 East Mill Street
Elora, ON N0B 1S0
1-877-242-6353
elora.info

The Gorge Cinema is one of the oldest — if not *the* oldest — continuously running rep cinemas in Canada. It is located in the historic Commercial Hotel building and combines state-of-the-art digital projection with rustic charm.

The Elora Festival, featuring the Festival Singers, is an annual celebration of music that attracts world-class performers of classical, gospel, jazz, blues and other genres. Performances take place in local churches and at the hall-like Gambrel Barn on County Road 18. The festival's lineup has included Canadian luminaries such as Maureen Forrester, Ben Heppner, Holly Cole, Sarah McLachlan, Jesse Cook, Moe Koffman and Andre Laplante, as well as international stars like Dame Cleo Laine and Dame Kiri te Kanawa.

The village's other music festival, Riverfest Elora, is held along the banks of the Grand River. This three-day, three-stage festival has featured such performers as Chromeo, Metric, Blue Rodeo, Sam Roberts Band, The Sheepdogs, Sharon Jones & the Dap-Kings, 54-40, Bahamas, Tokyo Police Club and Yukon Blonde.

Of course, many are attracted to Elora not for its historic limestone buildings, boutiques and arts festivals but for the prehistoric 24-metre (80 ft) limestone cliffs of the Gorge. Found at the west end of the village, the Elora Gorge Conservation Area (operated by the Grand River Conservation Authority) offers canoeing, kayaking, paddleboating, tubing, hiking, fishing and camping. The Elora Gorge is one of the most spectacular natural areas in the Grand River Val-

ley. Riverside trails and scenic overlooks offer hikers stunning views of the river far below. At the east end of the village, the Elora Quarry Conservation Area, a scenic former limestone quarry, is a popular swimming area.

Outdoor enthusiasts can cycle a portion of The Great Trail (formerly known as the Trans-Canada Trail) that links Elora with other rural communities. Follow the many walking trails through the village and the Gorge area, explore the cliffs and caves, kayak, travel down the Grand River on your watercraft of choice, zip line across the Gorge or enjoy a leisurely hot-air balloon ride over some of the most compelling scenery in southern Ontario.

FACING PAGE: The Grand River drops, narrows and picks up speed as it passes the Elora Mill and straddles the Tooth of Time. BELOW: The Wall of Doors, the famous sidewall of the shop Mermaid in Elora on Metcalfe Street.

14 OXFORD COUNTY CHEESE TRAIL

～ Ingersoll, Woodstock & Bright

At the peak of Oxford's dairy days, the county was home to 98 cheese factories. Although far fewer factories dot the picturesque rural landscape today, Oxford producers still make more than 70 varieties of cheese and dairy products.

At the Ingersoll Cheese & Agricultural Museum, visitors can learn about the area's more than 150 years of cheese making. Exhibits in seven on-site buildings tell the story of Ingersoll from its pioneer days to its modern-day home on the cheese trail. Tours are available with guides who are glad to spin tales of the town's cheese history — including the 3,311-kilogram (7,300 lb) cheese wheel of 1866. Behind the museum, in Centennial Park, there's a cheese-themed playground and a quiet place to have a picnic of cheese purchased in the museum.

The four unique artisanal producers on the Cheese Tour are Gunn's Hill Artisan Cheese, Mountainoak Cheese, Quality Sheep Milk Ltd. and Amarjit Singh's Local Dairy.

Gunn's Hill Artisan Cheese is a small cheese plant nestled in the rolling hills along Gunn's Hill Road, just south of Woodstock. Owner, operator and cheese-maker Shep Ysselstein produces truly unique cheeses with a Swiss influence. (He trained in the Swiss Alps.) The milk used to make Gunn's Hill artisan cheeses comes from the Holsteins living next door at Friesvale Farms, a third-generation family farm operated by Shep's father and brother. Gunn's Hill has won numerous awards, including the Canadian Cheese Grand Prix for their famous Five Brothers and Handeck cheeses.

In 1976, owners Adam and Hannie van Bergeijk took over the family dairy farm in Holland and attended cheese-making school in Gouda. After 20 years and several cheese

TOP LEFT: Curious goats at Quality Sheep Milk Ltd., makers of fine sheep- and goat-milk cheeses. LEFT: Cheese-makers (left to right) from Gunn's Hill Artisan Cheese, Local Dairy Products, Mountainoak Cheese and Bright Cheese & Butter.

CLOCKWISE FROM TOP LEFT: Elm Hurst Inn & Spa, on the site where James Harris made his famous 3,311-kilogram (7,300 lb) "Mammoth Cheese" in 1866; employees tend the vats at Bright Cheese & Butter, in Bright; hoisting a wheel at Gunn's Hill Artisan Cheese, south of Woodstock.

Things to See & Do

- Visit the Ingersoll Cheese & Agricultural Museum.
- Try the award-winning Five Brothers cheese at Gunn's Hill Artisan Cheese.
- Compare 16 goudas at Mountainoak Cheese.
- Sample Amarjit Singh's gold-star Mexican cheese.

Tourism Oxford
580 Bruin Boulevard
Woodstock, ON
N4V 1E5
519-539-9800
Ext. 3355
1-866-801-7368
tourismoxford.ca/
   cheese-trail

industry awards, the couple moved to Canada to continue and expand their craft. Their Mountainoak Cheese is a state-of-the-art facility that uses only milk from their own herd. They produce over 16 kinds of goudas, including black truffle, wild nettle and their award-winning Farmstead Premium Dutch gold and smoked varieties.

Operated by Ellis, Hazel and Sion Morris, Quality Sheep Milk Ltd. produces delicious sheep's-milk cheeses on its 52-hectare (128 acres) sheep and dairy goat farm. Among Quality Sheep Milk Ltd.'s fine cheeses are its Italian-style pecorino and the Trail's only feta.

For over two decades, Amarjit Singh and family have been producing artisanal, all-natural dairy products out of a historic cheese factory in Ingersoll. Although their company is called Local Dairy, its range of cheeses is international. Singh learned to make Indian-style cheese from his mother. Since then, he has created more than 20 unique dairy products, including his Canadian Cheese Grand Prix-winning Oaxaca (a semi-firm string cheese traditionally found in southern Mexico). Local Dairy is also known for its paneer, crème fraiche, ghee, koch kase, dulce de leche and cajeta caramel, produced under its Asli, La Vaquita and Perth County brands.

On a larger scale, Bright Cheese & Butter dates back to 1874, when a group of local farmers used their surplus milk to create a cheese factory with an emphasis on cheddar. By the turn of the century, Bright Cheese had become Canada's number-two exporter of cheddar, leading to the establishment of 1,242 cheddar factories in Ontario. Over 140 years later, the company still produces award-winning cheeses at its 19th-century factory in Bright, Ontario.

15 POINT PELEE NATIONAL PARK
~ Leamington

Welcome to the southernmost point of mainland Canada, a less than 10-kilometre (6.2 mi) spit of land jutting out into Lake Erie, its terminus equal in latitude to California's northern border. It is one of Canada's smallest but most diverse national parks, with marsh and dryland habitats, red cedar savannah and jungle-like swamp forest, and beaches that appear and disappear with the lake's winds and currents.

Naturally, birds of all shapes and sizes are attracted by these Airbnb options, which make Point Pelee a birder's paradise. The peninsula is located at the crossroads of two major migration routes that extend into the western basin of Lake Erie. It is one of the first points of land that spring-migration birds reach in the pre-dawn hours after crossing Lake Erie during the night.

The end of April brings the first wave of songbirds. Visit during the first three weeks of May to see the greatest diversity of songbirds. Forty-two of the 55 regularly occurring warbler species in North America have been recorded at Point Pelee.

FACING PAGE: The floating marsh boardwalk leads visitors on a 45-minute walk through the park's most diverse habitat. BELOW: Point Pelee is a migratory hot spot for birds as well as the monarch butterfly, which stops off on its way to points south.

Indeed, Point Pelee National Park has been called "the park the birds built." Over the past 100 years, 347 bird species have been recorded here. Nearly 100 species nest here, and about 50 overwinter. Dead trees provide nesting sites for tree swallows, wrens, wood ducks, woodpeckers, great horned owls and the prothonotary warbler. The fields fill with meadowlarks, field sparrows, rufous-sided towhees, wood pee-wees, red-eyed vireos and yellow-billed cuckoos, while the beaches host gulls, crows and grackles. Among the rarer species are the Virginia warbler, lesser nighthawk, swallow-tailed kite, sage thrasher and Cassin's sparrow.

In May, the Friends of Point Pelee hold an annual Festival of Birds, which features informative Intro to Birding hikes, Spring Migration Photography Walks and learning sessions on songbirds, shorebirds and hawks, led by top naturalists and ornithologists.

In autumn, the songbirds dart in and out of the vegetation as dragonflies and monarch butterflies migrate their own routes. Other park wildlife

FACING PAGE: Cedar waxwings typically winter farther south, but this one has joined the 50 species that now overwinter in the park, thanks to global warming. ABOVE: The park is home to bullfrogs, green frogs, spring peepers, western chorus frogs, northern leopard frogs and six turtle species.

Things to See & Do

- Visit the park during the Festival of Birds.
- Keep a species count.
- Paddle through the lush marshland.
- Plan a Dark Sky night.

Point Pelee National Park
1118 Point Pelee Drive
Leamington, ON
N8H 3V4
519-322-2365
1-888-773-8888
pc.gc.ca/en/pn-np/on/
   pelee

includes the grey squirrel, raccoon, weasel, mink, skunk, coyote, the reintroduced southern flying squirrel, several species of bat, the bullfrog, green frog, spring peeper, western chorus frog, northern leopard frog, six species of turtle, and a few non-poisonous snakes.

More than 700 species of flowering and non-flowering plants live here. In dry forest areas, the southern hackberry, ropelike wild grape, Virginia creeper and poison ivy vines create a jungle effect. The grasslands produce rare grasses, wild potato vine and prickly pear cactus.

If you like being on the move, you can canoe or kayak the marshlands, stroll the boardwalk or walk the sandy beach. The park also has more than 12 kilometres (7.5 mi) of trails.

If plants and wildlife and birds aren't your thing, look a bit further. Point Pelee has been designated a Dark Sky Preserve by the Windsor Centre of the Royal Astronomical Society of Canada, and the park calendar includes Dark Sky nights for both knowledgeable and novice astronomers.

16

RIVERFRONT TRAIL & SCULPTURE PARK
∽ Windsor

Tembo, the Swahili word for elephant, is the title of Derrick Stephan Hudson's bronze sculpture of an elephant mother trailed by two young. Each year, the City of Windsor encourages residents to participate in the washing of the sculpture on *Tembo* Day.

From its starting point in Assumption Park, beside the Ambassador Bridge, Windsor's scenic Riverfront Trail runs for eight kilometres (5 mi) northeast along the Detroit River to Lincoln Avenue, passing through Ambassador Park, the Windsor Sculpture Park, Centennial Park, Dieppe Gardens, the Riverfront Festival Plaza, Bert Weeks Memorial Gardens and the Joan and Clifford Hatch Wildflower Garden.

Ambassador Park is actually a three-part park that includes Assumption Park and Centennial Park. Pedestrians and cyclists can follow a park path called the Roy Battagello Riverwalk through the eclectic Windsor Sculpture Park (formerly the Odette Sculpture Park).

The Windsor Sculpture Park contains 35 large-scale contemporary sculptures by renowned artists such as Elisabeth Frink, Gerald Gladstone and Sorel Etrog. The sculptures range from realistic to abstract to whimsical, unified only by their size and diversity — a dinosaur, a canoe with voyageurs, a pipe-lined audio corridor, a giant egg, a dancing bear, stylized Catholic sisters, *Space Plough 2* and *Penguins on a Waterfall*. Also among the sculptures is Derrick Stephan Hudson's large bronze *Tembo*, a mother elephant with two tiny offspring. On *Tembo* Day each year, the Windsor residents are encouraged to participate in the washing of *Tembo*. The Windsor Sculpture Park stretches from Assumption Park to Centennial Park and was funded by Mr. and Mrs. Louis Odette.

As its name implies, Centennial Park officially opened on July 1, 1967. A time capsule sealed that day will be opened in 2067. The park's walking and cycling trails offer excellent views of the river.

Dieppe Gardens, at 78 Riverside Drive West, were created in memory of the many members of the Essex–Kent Scottish Regiment who lost their lives during the 1942 Dieppe landing. The park is planted with brilliantly coloured annuals and perennials and features a waterfall and fish pond, as well as numerous military monuments.

Past the Detroit–Windsor Tunnel is the Riverfront Festival Plaza, the site for many of the city's popular outdoor festivals, concerts and events. Linking the Festival Plaza on the west to the Joan and Clifford Hatch Wildflower Garden on the east is Bert Weeks Memorial Gardens, named in honour of former mayor Albert Howard "Bert" Weeks (in office from 1975 to 1982), who made it his mission to protect the riverfront from development. Among the highlights of the Memorial Gardens is an elaborate fountain with a reflecting pool.

The Joan and Clifford Hatch Wildflower Garden, at the eastern end of the Riverfront Trail, is named for two noted philanthropists. It is located in a historically significant area that was home to the Ottawa First Nation prior to 1730. They were followed by the French, the British and the United Empire Loyalists. The Wildflower Garden layout echoes the current of the Detroit River. With an emphasis on native plants and wildflowers, it is designed to be self-sustaining and to provide enhanced fish habitat.

Things to See & Do

- Walk or cycle the eight-kilometre Riverfront Trail.
- Take your camera with you to the Sculpture Park.
- Spend time among the monuments and memorials at Dieppe Gardens.
- Enjoy the natural beauty of the Wildflower Garden.

Tourism Windsor Essex Pelee Island
333 Riverside Drive West, Suite 103
Windsor, ON N9A 7C5
1-800-265-3633
visitwindsoressex.com/ riverwalk

BELOW LEFT: With the Detroit skyline in background, *Claim Post* by Scott McKay leans toward Windsor, ribbons representing creative energy, the blue post representing strength of community. BELOW RIGHT: *King and Queen* by Sorel Etrog considers the relationship between man and machinery.

17

SALMON TOUR &
TOM THOMSON ART GALLERY
∼ Owen Sound

Chinook salmon are native to the Pacific Ocean, but they were introduced to the Great Lakes in the 1960s to control the invasive alewife (a species of herring) population. The Chinook took a liking to the cool waters of Georgian Bay. Each year, Owen Sound's Sydenham Sportsmen, a non-profit conservation group, raises and releases up to 500,000 salmon and trout into the Sydenham River. Their Weaver's Creek hatchery is spring-fed and stays cool enough year-round for the fish to hatch and grow. In spring, when they reach the smolt (juvenile) stage, they are released into the Sydenham River and navigate their way to Georgian Bay. They live there for the next three to four years, until fully mature, before returning to spawn in the river from whence they came.

Owen Sound is among the few places in Ontario where you can watch these colourful, determined salmon spawn before migrating upstream to lay their eggs before winter. The weather-dependent salmon run defies the calendar but typi-

Owen Sound is among the few places in the province where you can watch the upstream migration, thanks to the efforts of the Sydenham Sportsmen, who constructed the first fish ladder in Ontario to assist spawning salmon.

CLOCKWISE FROM TOP LEFT: The Tom Thomson Art Gallery features the artist's work and memorabilia; jumping fish are fun for the whole family; the mill dam and fish ladder are cooperatively run by the Ministry of Natural Resources, the Sydenham Sportsmen and the Grey–Sauble Conservation Authority.

cally extends from mid-September to mid-October. On October 1, the city holds a special Salmon Celebration.

When they venture upstream on the Sydenham River, the salmon encounter a former mill dam. It would be impossible for the fish to scale were it not for a fish ladder alongside it built by the Sydenham Sportsmen in 1967 — the first fish ladder in Ontario. The mill dam and fish ladder are cooperatively run by the Ministry of Natural Resources, the Sydenham Sportsmen and the Grey–Sauble Conservation Authority. The Sportsmen have also worked with the Conservation Authority to create spawning channels at various points along the river.

The Salmon Tour route follows a mostly paved path along the harbourfront in downtown Owen Sound, then along packed-dirt walkways and paved trails in Harrison Park and more rugged paths to the spawning channels of Grey–Sauble Conservation and Inglis Falls. The walking tour is about five kilometres (3 mi). Along the route, you'll see the harbourfront, the Tom Thomson Art Gallery, the Owen Sound Farmers' Market and "Millionaire's Drive," with its historic homes backing onto the Sydenham River.

The Tom Thomson Art Gallery is an excellent diversion. The gallery features a renowned collection of artwork and memorabilia by Tom Thomson, the iconic Canadian painter who grew up in nearby Leith and who inspired the Group of Seven. (Thomson's grave is in Leith cemetery behind the old church on Tom Thomson Road.)

The Tom Thomson Art Gallery holds a collection of more than 2,300 works — paintings, drawings, prints, photographs, sculptures and crafts. Beyond the masterful works by Tom Thomson and the Group of Seven, the collection focuses on significant contemporary art by regional and national artists who work in the landscape tradition. ✑

Things to See & Do

- Walk the Salmon Tour route along the harbourfront.
- Watch the salmon climb the fish ladder en route to spawning.
- View the gallery's fine collection of Thomson paintings.
- Discover new Canadian artists working in the landscape tradition.

Owen Sound Tourism
1155 First Avenue West
Owen Sound, ON
N4K 4K8
519-371-9833
1-888-675-5555
owensoundtourism.ca
tomthomson.org

18

SIX NATIONS OF THE GRAND RIVER

~ Ohsweken

BELOW: The Six Nations community gathers each June for Indigenous People's Day and in late July for the colourful Champion of Champions Pow Wow. FACING PAGE: Built in 1785 by the Crown and gifted to the Loyalist First Nations, the Mohawk Chapel is the oldest surviving church in Ontario.

The Six Nations of the Grand River (Six Nations) is the most populous reserve in Canada, with more than 25,600 band members, approximately 12,270 of whom live on the reserve. It is located approximately 25 kilometres (15½ mi) southwest of Hamilton, between the cities of Brantford, Caledonia and Hagersville.

Six Nations is an active Haudenosaunee community. The Haudenosaunee Confederacy comprises six member nations: the Onondaga, Cayuga, Mohawk, Oneida, Seneca and Tuscarora, and this is the only place in North America where all six Haudenosaunee nations live together. Haudenosaunee translates as "They Build Houses." In the 18th and 19th centuries, up to 20 families, all related matrilineally, lived in enormous structures called "longhouses." A typical longhouse was about 24.4 by 5.5 by 5.5 metres (80x18x18 ft), and several of these buildings created cities in the middle of wilderness.

The Haudenosaunee Confederacy is also known as the Iroquois League. According to Haudenosaunee beliefs, the alliance was formed during ancient times by a man known as the Peacemaker. With a powerful mind and a superhuman ability to positively influence people, the Peacemaker brought peace to the Haudenosaunee by changing minds, subverting constant war and chaos and uniting the people in a spiritual-political system called the Great Law. The Great Law system organizes families into clans, with clan identify passed down through the mother. The Haudenosaunee were and still are matrilineal. Each clan family has a chief and a clan mother, whose responsibilities include taking care of the law and serving the people.

On the Six Nations Grand River territory, you'll find the descendants of the original Haudenosaunee continuing their ceremonies and preserving their language and culture — all within a short drive of bustling southern Ontario cities. Visitors can canoe the Grand River, hike the trails, explore the work of skilled craftspeople and discover the story of the Haudenosaunee, who inhabited these lands hundreds of years before the first European came ashore.

Chiefswood National Historic Site features a combination of habitat — rare grassland prairie, Carolinian forest, wetlands and, of course, the Grand River. It is against this glorious natural backdrop that the Six Nations community gathers each June for Indigenous Peoples' Day and in late July for the colourful Champion of Champions Pow Wow.

From May to November, or by request, you can visit Chiefswood mansion. The birthplace of famed Mohawk-English poet Pauline Johnson, stately Chiefswood was built by her father, a hereditary clan chief, in the mid-1850s. The house features two front doors: One faces the river to welcome Mohawks who arrived by canoe, and one faces the road to welcome the English who arrived by buggy from early Brantford.

The Mohawk Chapel is located along the Grand River on Six Nations land within Brantford. Built in 1785, Her Majesty's Royal Chapel of the Mohawks is the last remaining building of the original Mohawk Village and the oldest surviving church in Ontario. Eight stained-glass windows designed by artist David Mitson depict significant historical events for Six Nations people. The chapel is also a National Historic Site.

Things to See & Do

- Attend the Champion of Champions Pow Wow.
- Discover the work of top Haudenosaunee craftspeople.
- Visit stately . Chiefswood mansion.
- Tour the Mohawk Chapel.

Six Nations Tourism
2498 Chiefswood Road
P.O. Box 569
Ohsweken, ON
N0A 1M0
519-758-5444
1-866-393-3001
sixnationstourism.ca

19

THE STRATFORD FESTIVAL
∿ Stratford

When the railway industry left Stratford in the early 1950s, journalist Tom Patterson proposed founding a Shakespearean theatre festival to boost the local economy. After all, this was Stratford, and the river over there was the Avon.

Stratford City Council gave Patterson $125 to seek artistic advice from theatre contacts in New York, where he hoped to meet with Laurence Olivier. That didn't pan out, but Canadian theatre pioneer Dora Mavor Moore soon put Patterson in touch with legendary British director Tyrone Guthrie. Intrigued, Guthrie visited Stratford to see if Patterson's idea might just work. Guthrie stayed, becoming the festival's first artistic director.

The Stratford Festival is now North America's largest classical repertory theatre company. Though the festival's primary mandate is to present Shakespeare's plays, its range has expanded over the years to accommodate audience demands. Currently, each season brings more than a dozen new productions — theatrical classics, contemporary dramas and musicals and, of course, the plays of Shakespeare. These are performed in four distinctive venues: the Festival Theatre, Avon Theatre, Tom Patterson Theatre and Studio Theatre. The festival runs from April to October, and street location, seating maps and virtual tours of each theatre are available on the Stratford Festival website.

The award-winning actors, both past and present, who have performed at the festival are myriad. They include Alan Bates, Brian Bedford, Jackie Burroughs, Zoe Caldwell, Hume Cronyn, Brian Dennehy, Colm Feore, Megan Follows, Lorne Greene, Paul Gross, Alec Guinness, Uta Hagen, Julie Harris, Martha Henry, William Hutt, Frances Hyland, James Mason, John Neville, Amanda Plummer, Christopher Plummer, Sarah Polley, Kate Reid, Jason Robards, Paul Scofield, William Shatner, Maggie Smith, Jessica Tandy and Peter Ustinov. Oh, and a young Christopher Walken, who played Romeo in the festival's 1968 production of *Romeo and Juliet*.

The Stratford Festival Forum runs during the season, featuring music concerts, timely lectures and readings from major authors. In spring, Stratford hosts the annual Swan Parade and the SpringWorks Indie Arts Festival. The highlight of summer is the festival itself, but it's worth investigating the Summer Music and Savour Stratford Culinary festivals. ∿

Things to See & Do

- See the Bard's work at its best.
- Discover a rising star.
- Attend performances at all four theatres.
- Check out the SpringWorks Indie Arts Festival.

Box Office
55 Queen Street
Stratford, ON N5A 4M9
519-273-1600
1-800-567-1600
stratfordfestival.ca

CLOCKWISE FROM LEFT: There is plenty of upscale shopping and dining in downtown Stratford; the Festival Theatre Stage; exterior, Stratford's main venue, the Festival Theatre.

CENTRAL
ONTARIO

TORONTO

20 ∼ Aga Khan Museum & Ismaili Centre |
   North York
21 ∼ Art Gallery of Ontario | Toronto
22 ∼ BAPS Shri Swaminarayan Mandir |
   Etobicoke
23 ∼ Bata Shoe Museum | Toronto
24 ∼ Canadian National Exhibition &
   Royal Agricultural Winter Fair | Toronto
25 ∼ Casa Loma & Spadina Museum | Toronto
26 ∼ Chinatown | Toronto
27 ∼ CN Tower | Toronto
28 ∼ The Distillery Historic District | Toronto
29 ∼ High Park | Toronto
30 ∼ Hockey Hall of Fame | Toronto
31 ∼ Massey Hall & Roy Thomson Hall |
   Toronto
32 ∼ Royal Ontario Museum | Toronto
33 ∼ St. Lawrence Market | Toronto
34 ∼ Toronto Caribbean Carnival Parade |
   Toronto
35 ∼ Toronto Pride Festival & Parade | Toronto
36 ∼ The Word On The Street | Toronto

37 ∼ Ball's Falls & Cataract Trail |
   Jordan/Ball's Falls
38 ∼ Brock's Monument & Historic Fort George |
   Queenston Heights

39 ∼ Canada's Largest Ribfest vs. North America's
   Largest Vegetarian Food Festival |
   Burlington/Toronto
40 ∼ Canada's Wonderland | Vaughan
41 ∼ Canadian Warplane Heritage Museum |
   Hamilton/Mount Hope
42 ∼ City of Waterfalls | Hamilton
43 ∼ Cobourg Beach & Sandcastle Festival |
   Cobourg
44 ∼ Halton County Radial Railway Museum |
   Milton
45 ∼ Halton High Points | Mount Nemo,
   Rattlesnake Point, Kelso, Crawford Lake &
   Hilton Falls
46 ∼ Hiking Headwaters Country | Erin, Caledon
   & Dufferin County
47 ∼ McMichael Canadian Art Collection |
   Kleinburg
48 ∼ Niagara-on-the-Lake Historic District
   & the Shaw Festival | Niagara-on-the-Lake
49 ∼ Niagara Falls | Niagara Falls
50 ∼ Niagara Wine Country | Niagara Peninsula
51 ∼ "Ontario's Best-Preserved Main Street" |
   Port Hope
52 ∼ Remembrance Park |
   Georgetown/Halton Hills
53 ∼ Royal Botanical Gardens | Burlington
54 ∼ Sound of Music Festival | Burlington

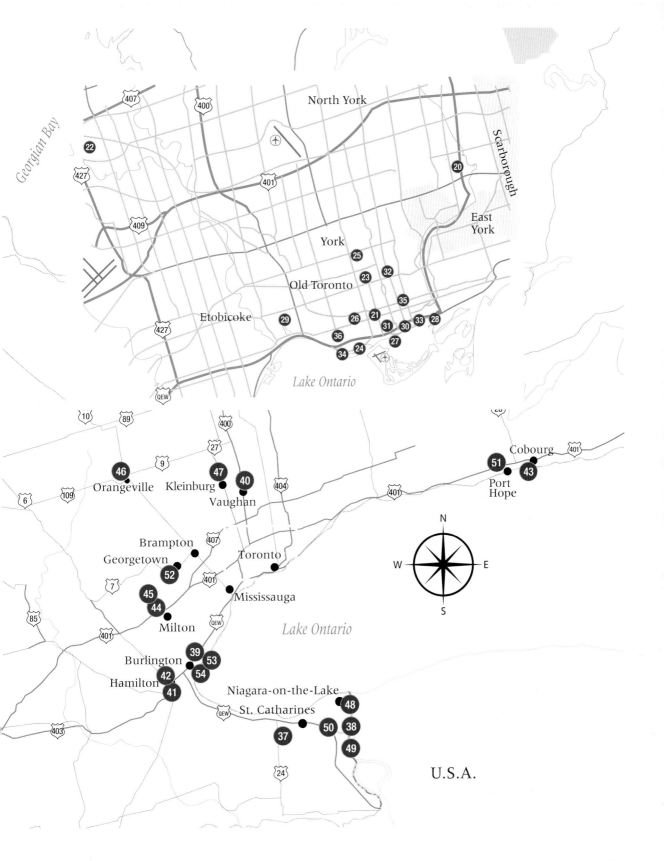

20 AGA KHAN MUSEUM & ISMAILI CENTRE, TORONTO
∾ North York

The Aga Khan Museum offers visitors "a window into worlds unknown or unfamiliar: the artistic, intellectual and scientific heritage of Muslim civilizations across the centuries, from the Iberian Peninsula to China."

Award-winning architect Fumihiko Maki designed the museum to ensure that light is ever-present in the building — according to the weather and the time of day or season, light animates the building with patterns, beams and shadows. The result incorporates historical elements of Islamic cultures into a distinctly contemporary design.

At 81 metres (266 ft) long and 54 metres (177 ft) wide, the modestly sized museum makes efficient use of space, with two exhibition galleries, areas for art conservation and storage, a 350-seat theatre and two classrooms. The museum's permanent collection holds over 1,000 artifacts and works of art dating from the 8th century through the 21st century, ranging in origin from Spain to Southeast

LEFT: Artist Minaz Nanji's *99 Names of Allah*, created using tiger's eye, lapis lazuli and other gemstones, appears in the Ismaili Centre, Toronto. BELOW: The towering glass roof of the Ismaili Centre's prayer hall.

The exterior of the Aga Khan Museum is reflected in one of its five granite-lined pools. The museum was designed to ensure that light is ever-present in the relatively small building.

Things to See & Do

- Discover centuries of Muslim culture in the museum's permanent collection.
- Attend a full schedule of music and dance performances.
- Enjoy the tranquility of Aga Khan Park and the Ismaili Centre, Toronto.

Aga Khan Museum
77 Wynford Drive
North York, ON M3C 1K1
416-646-4677
agakhanmuseum.org

Ismaili Centre, Toronto
49 Wynford Drive
North York, ON M3C 1K1
416-646-6965
theismaili.org

Asia. Arranged by media — manuscripts, drawings and paintings, decorated ceramics, metalwork, architectural ornamentation, garments, tapestries — these works offer an awe-inspiring look at the arts and culture of Islamic civilizations throughout the ages.

The Aga Khan Museum also maintains a vibrant series of travelling exhibitions, lectures, workshops, films, music and dance performances, and community events. As part of its international mandate, it works closely with such institutions as the Louvre in Paris, France, the State Hermitage Museum in St. Petersburg, Russia, and the Museum of Islamic Art in Doha, Qatar.

Adjacent to the Aga Khan Museum is the futuristic-looking Ismaili Centre, Toronto. Designed by acclaimed Indian architect Charles Correa, the centre combines spacious rooms for social events with designated areas for spiritual reflection and prayer. Its domed roof features crystalline frosted glass and is the highest point on the grounds, which span 6.8 hectares (17 acres).

Like the Ismaili centres in Vancouver, London, Lisbon, Dubai and Dushanbe, the Ismaili Centre, Toronto hosts programs that "stimulate the intellect, encourage dialogue, and celebrate cultural diversity." The centre seeks to create an understanding of the values, culture and heritage of Ismaili Muslims and of the work of the Aga Khan Development Network.

The Aga Khan Park, which connects the centre with the museum, was designed by Lebanese landscape architect Vladimir Djurovic and is a place for peaceful reflection, highlighted by five pools and formal gardens.

21

ART GALLERY OF ONTARIO
～ Toronto

The Art Gallery of Ontario (AGO) is home to the world's largest collection of Canadian art. In fact, at least half of the AGO's collection of 90,000 works are by Canadian artists, among them the Group of Seven, Tom Thomson, Emily Carr, Cornelius Krieghoff, Betty Goodwin, David Blackwood, David Milne and Inuit and Indigenous artists Kenojuak Ashevak, Norval Morrisseau and Jackson Beardy.

The gallery's impressive collection of European art includes major works by Tintoretto, Bernini, Rubens, Rembrandt, Gainsborough, Van Dyck, Goya and Bourdelle, as well as works by Picasso, Rodin, Pissarro, Monet, Toulouse-Lautrec, Bonnard, Dufy, Cézanne, Tissot, Sisley and Degas.

Its modern and contemporary collection traces the evolution of artistic movements in Canada, the United States and Europe, with works by Kline, Rothko, Gorky, Miró, Chagall, Matisse, Modigliani, Tanguy, Dalí, O'Keeffe, Kurelek, Hepworth, Riopelle, Snow, Chambers and Canadian conceptualist trio General Idea. The contemporary collection includes installa-

ABOVE: The gallery's sculptural round staircase, designed by architect Frank Gehry, integrates with the courtyard of the existing baroque building.
RIGHT: In the gallery's renovation and expansion, Gehry combined the historic Victorian mansion with a bold modern addition.

Art Gallery of Ontario

ABOVE: Henry Moore's sculpture *Two Large Forms* provides an abstract welcome to the AGO. RIGHT: The new Galleria Italia wing is situated above the entry to the AGO and allows visitors to experience the surrounding cityscape.

Things to See & Do

- See the world's largest collection of Canadian art.
- Discover old and modern masters.
- Visit the Henry Moore Sculpture Centre.
- Marvel at Frank Gehry's AGO transformation.

Art Gallery of Ontario
317 Dundas Street West
Toronto, ON M5T 1G4
1-877-225-4246
416-979-6648
ago.net

tions, photography, graphic art, posters, film and video.

With more than 40,000 works, the AGO's photography collection contains both historical and contemporary works by the likes of Brassaï, Edward Burtynsky, Julia Margaret Cameron, Walker Evans, Larry Fink and Robert J. Flaherty. It also has one of North America's most significant collections of African art and the largest collection of Oceanic art and artifacts in Canada. Among the gallery's many highlights is the Henry Moore Sculpture Centre, which holds the world's largest public collection of Moore's work, most of it donated by the artist in the early 1970s.

In 2002, media baron and philanthropist Ken Thomson donated much of his private art collection to the AGO, along with $50 million toward the gallery's renovation and expansion (Transformation AGO) and a $20-million endowment. The architectural expansion — by world-renowned architect Frank Gehry — was completed in 2008 and remains one of North America's most critically acclaimed architectural achievements.

22

BAPS SHRI SWAMINARAYAN MANDIR
～ Etobicoke

The BAPS Shri Swaminarayan Mandir rises from the surrounding suburban landscape like an outsized ivory carving or an ethereal wedding cake — a delightful architectural surprise as one heads north of Finch Avenue on Highway 427. This temple of Hindu faith and culture is the largest in Canada and was built in just 18 months with more than 24,000 blocks of Italian marble, Turkish limestone and stone sourced from India.

The mandir was constructed according to the principles of the Shilpa Shastras (ancient Hindu rules of craft and design). Skilled craftsmen hand-carved each block of stone, including the five amazingly intricate shrines to the Murti, which represent the sacred deities. The mandir is open daily to visitors and for worship. Because it is a meditation area, visitors are asked to maintain respectful silence.

At 7.3 hectares (18 acres), the grounds feature a cultural centre (the Haveli) and a heritage museum. The courtyard inside the Haveli is surrounded by teak and rosewood columns ornately carved with images of mythological animals and

Things to See & Do

- Watch multimedia presentations on the building of the mandir.
- Admire the amazing hand-carved stone architecture.
- Visit the mandir's five ornate shrines.
- Learn about the rich heritage of Indo-Canadians.

BAPS Shri
  Swaminarayan Mandir
61 Claireville Drive
Etobicoke, ON
M9W 5Z7
416-798-2277
baps.org/Global-
  Network/North-
  America/Toronto.aspx

A closeup of the detailed carving that decorates Etobicoke's BAPS Shri Swaminarayan Mandir, or Hindu temple.

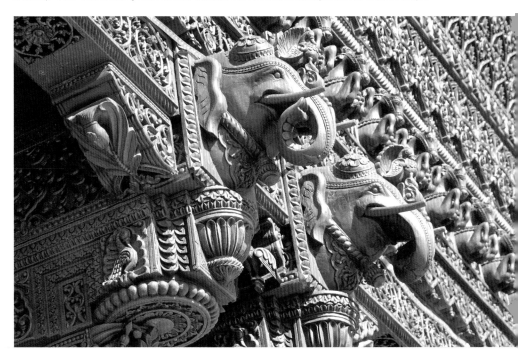

figures. The cultural centre houses an assembly hall, classrooms for educational activities and music lessons, a full-sized gymnasium and a vegetarian food shop.

The heritage museum's exhibits explain the ancient origins and key tenets of Hinduism but also highlight the important contributions Indo-Canadians have made in the fields of art, architecture, science, education, multicultural-ism, politics and spiritual values.

BAPS is the abbreviation for Bochasanwasi Akshar Purushottam Sanstha, a global reli-gious and civic organization within the Swaminarayan branch of Hinduism. The BAPS Swaminarayan Mandir of Toronto holds an annual gala to raise awareness and support for charities. Past beneficiaries include the Canadian National Institute for the Blind, the Heart and Stroke Foundation and organizations involved in rebuilding efforts following the natural disasters in Haiti and Japan. Alongside BAPS centres throughout North America, the BAPS Mandir of Toronto hosts an annual char-ity walkathon, an annual health fair and an annual conference in support of International Women's Day.

TOP: Described as a masterpiece of intricate design and workman-ship, Etobicoke's BAPS Shri Swaminarayan Mandir complex features the province's first traditional hand-carved Hindu place of worship. ABOVE: Life-sized figures are carved into the building's walls.

23

BATA SHOE MUSEUM
∼ Toronto

Located at the corner of Bloor and St. George streets in downtown Toronto, the Bata Shoe Museum is hard to miss. Its smooth five-storey walls, made of hand-selected French limestone, reach out to passersby at sleek, canted angles. Designed by architect Raymond Moriyama, the building is not unlike an alluring, oversized postmodern shoebox.

Museum founder Sonja Bata began collecting shoes in the 1940s, gradually assembling what is perhaps the planet's most comprehensive collection of ancient and modern footwear. The 3,622-square-metre (39,000 sq ft) building houses over 13,000 artifacts spanning 4,500 years of history.

The museum's archaeological collection features original renderings and

RIGHT: The Standing Tall exhibit includes platform shoes and high-heeled boots worn by rock-and-roll royalty. BELOW, LEFT TO RIGHT: Italian footwear, c.1700; Chinese footwear, c. 1870–1900; North American Native footwear, c. 1880; 17th-century Persian footwear; white reindeer-skin boots with woven ties, Aiddejavre, Norway.

The Bata Shoe Museum's postmodern exterior at the corner of Bloor and St. George.

representations of footwear from some of the earliest civilizations and includes ancient Egyptian and Roman sandal designs and medieval footwear. How about French chestnut-crushing boots, a Japanese samurai's bear-fur shoes or a precariously high velvet-covered platform mule from 16th-century Italy?

The museum's mission is "to contribute to the knowledge and understanding of the role of footwear in the social and cultural life of humanity." The Bata Museum allows us to look beyond our current desire for the perfect heel, pump or sneaker to appreciate the part footwear's form, functionality and style play in our ongoing cultural evolution.

Bata's thousands of artfully displayed shoes chronicle centuries of change in the way various cultures around the globe live — the role of climate, fluctuating societal values, matters of gender identity and social status and, most recently, advanced materials and manufacturing technology.

An important draw among the museum's holdings is its extensive collection of Native American and circumpolar footwear, but we live in a culture of celebrity, so even the most outlandish historic footwear must compete with Queen Victoria's ballroom slippers, Elvis Presley's blue patent loafers, John Lennon's Beatle boot, Elton John's silver platform boots, Terry Fox's running shoe and Karen Kain's ballet slippers.

Things to See & Do

- View Native American and circumpolar footwear.
- See celebrity footwear up close.
- Appreciate the evolution of sneakers.

Bata Shoe Museum
327 Bloor Street West
Toronto, ON
M5S 1W7
416-979-7799
batashoemuseum.ca

24

CANADIAN NATIONAL EXHIBITION & ROYAL AGRICULTURAL WINTER FAIR

∼ Toronto

BELOW: A winning contestant leads her well-groomed horse before the crowd at the Royal Winter Fair. FACING PAGE: An aerial view of the Canadian National Exhibition's midway at night.

First held in 1879, the Canadian National Exhibition (a.k.a. the CNE and the Ex) remains a major Toronto attraction and the place many Ontarians choose to wrap up their summer. The country's largest annual fair takes place during the 18 days leading up to and including Canada's Labour Day and draws more than 1.5 million visitors.

The first Canadian National Exhibition was staged to promote Canada's advancements in agriculture and technology, and that is a still part of the Exhibition's agenda, but most visitors come for the entertainment, the rides and the food.

The Crazy Mouse rollercoaster lights up the night at the CNE grounds.

The Ex is held at Exhibition Place, a collection of parks, large buildings (many historic), live music venues (including the CNE Bandshell) and BMO Field that encompasses 78 hectares (192 acres).

The 18-day fair offers nearly nonstop live entertainment, midway rides, carnival games, agricultural and food-related presentations, sporting contests, casino activity and stage, stunt and talent shows. The Canadian International Air Show, on Labour Day weekend, has been a CNE highlight since 1949.

The enormous Enercare Centre complex is home to the International Pavilion, the Garden Show and the popular SuperDogs performances. North of the Centre is the Ricoh Coliseum, where the high-wire acts and ice shows happen. And located beside the Coliseum, the Horse Palace hosts the hands-on HorseCapades and HorsePower Live!, a showcase of acrobatic riding and precision equestrian events. The Better Living Centre continues the CNE tradition of agricultural competitions, including an annual butter-sculpting competition.

Speaking of butter, the global novelty Deep-fried Butter debuted at the Ex in 2010. Many people associate the fair with eccentric, often highly caloric eats, and these aren't hard to come by — Frosted-Flake-Battered Chicken on a Stick, Spaghetti Doughnut Balls, Pancake Bacon Tacos, Deep-fried Red Velvet Oreos —

Synchronized aerial acrobatics at the Ex's Canadian International Air Show.

Things to See & Do

- Enjoy the final carnival midway of summer.
- Attend celebrity chef presentations.
- See the Canadian International Air Show.
- Come back in November for the Royal Horse Show.

Exhibition Place
210 Princes' Boulevard
Toronto, ON M6K 3C3
416-649-8780
1-844-398-3278
theex.com
royalfair.org

but the Food Building offers a wide range of healthier options, including halal and vegetarian meals. World-class chefs appear daily at Celebrity Chef Stage presentations, and in recent years, Food Truck Frenzy has been a hit along Princes' Boulevard. The Ex takes feeding its visitors seriously and maintains an online list of hundreds of items available for $5 or less.

The carnival midway offers thrill rides, rollercoasters, swing rides, a log plume ride, games of skill and chance, and more food. The Sky Ride carries riders from one end of the midway to the other in ski-lift-style chairs.

The Ex's country cousin, the Royal Agricultural Winter Fair (the Royal) takes place on Exhibition Place grounds over two weeks in November. Livestock breeders bring almost 6,000 animals to downtown Toronto for the Royal, including roughly 5,000 cattle, sheep, goats, pigs, rabbits and chickens, and more than 900 horses. The Burnbrae Food & Lifestyle Stage hosts local and international chef challenges, food sampling and entertaining and decorating demonstrations. The President's Choice Animal Theatre presents animals at work and play, including sheep-herding challenges, Goats on the Go, Spirit of the Horse, rabbit jumping and, once again, the SuperDogs. The Royal Horse Show has been a feature event since the fair's inception in 1922.

25

CASA LOMA &
SPADINA MUSEUM
∼ Toronto

Water surges from the formal fountain in front of Toronto's Gothic Revival-style Casa Loma.

Each year, more than 350,000 visitors tour "Toronto's castle," Casa Loma. The "castle" was built for financier Sir Henry Mill Pellatt, who purchased 25 lots for the purpose in 1903. Its architect was E. J. Lennox, whose work includes several city landmarks, including the Toronto Athletic Club, Old City Hall and the Bank of Toronto building at Yonge and Queen. Construction commenced in 1911, and more than 300 workers laboured for three years to finish the 98-room residence. With 6,010 square metres (64,700 sq ft) of floor space, Casa Loma was the largest private residence in Canada at the time and probably the most ostentatious.

Named for an Ojibwe word that means "hill," Spadina House has enjoyed a long history in the city of Toronto and now serves as a museum, a meeting place and a venue for functions such as weddings and other celebrations.

Things to See and Do

- Explore the four floors of "Toronto's castle."
- Check out Casa Loma's stable of vintage cars.
- Marvel at hectares of formal gardens at both sites.
- Learn how Torontonians lived during the early 20th century.

Casa Loma
1 Austin Terrace
Toronto, ON M5R 1X8
416-923-1171
casaloma.ca

Spadina Museum
285 Spadina Road
Toronto, ON M5R 2V5
416-392-6910
toronto.ca/explore-enjoy/history-art-culture/museums/spadina-museum

The main floor features a great hall, library, study, conservatory, serving room, dining room, smoking room, billiards room and the most ornately crafted room in the house, the Oak Room. The second floor consists of Sir Henry and Lady Pellatt's separate suites and bathrooms, as well as a guest room, the Windsor Room and the Round Room.

Most of the unfinished third floor serves as the Regimental Museum for the Queen's Own Rifles of Canada. Pellatt joined the regiment as a Rifleman, rose to the rank of Commanding Officer and was promoted to Major-General upon retirement. Much of the basement also went unfinished (a pool, bowling lanes, shooting range, gymnasium). An underground tunnel leads from the basement to the property's hunting lodge and to the stables. In the carriage room and garage is an exhibition of vintage cars from the early 1900s.

With gardens that sprawl across more than two hectares (5 acres), Casa Loma is a magnificent setting for special events and hosts over 250 private functions annually. Its grand architecture also makes it a choice location for films. Films such as *Chicago*, *X-Men* and *Scott Pilgrim vs. the World* were shot here.

At the top of the Baldwin Steps, next door to Casa Loma, is Spadina (pronounced Spa-deen-a) House, now Spadina Museum. The original property was purchased in 1866 by James Austin, the founder of the Dominion Bank and Consumers Gas. Austin and his descendants subdivided and sold much of the property, which included a large 1913 sale to the City of Toronto for the construction of the St. Clair Reservoir. Austin's granddaughter Anna Kathleen Thompson was the final member of the family to occupy Spadina House before donating the house and its furnishings to the city in 1982.

The Ontario Heritage Foundation and the City of Toronto opened the property as a museum in 1984. The historic manor's art, decor and architecture are preserved much as they appeared in the 1920s to 1930s. The estate's extensive gardens — 2.4 hectares (6 acres) that feature more than 300 varieties of plants — also echo the Austin family years.

26

CHINATOWN
～ Toronto

Although there are several active Chinese-Canadian communities in the Greater Toronto Area, the city's Old Chinatown, centred at the junction of Spadina Avenue and Dundas Street West, is now the second largest in North America (after San Francisco's historic Chinatown).

The densely concentrated community got its start in the late-19th-century squalor of the Ward (a downtown area bounded by College, Queen, Yonge and University) but began its migration west of city centre in the early 20th century. In recent decades, it has come to represent waves of immigration by members of many other East Asian cultures: Vietnamese, Korean and Thai shops and restaurants nestle between bustling Chinese businesses.

Two large Chinese malls, Dragon City (280 Spadina) and Chinatown Centre (222 Spadina), offer the mall experience with a decidedly Asian flair, but in good weather, visitors should roam the streets and take in the sounds and scents. Cured poultry is displayed on hooks in shop windows, and the fragrances of ginger, garlic, sesame, anise, fennel, chilies, soy and fish sauce fill the air. Animated vendors tend open-air stalls offering fresh (and sometimes exotic) fruits and vegetables, herbs, teapots, rice steamers, silks, linens, bamboo trinkets and teak souvenirs.

Seemingly hundreds of restaurants exist shoulder to shoulder and floor atop floor, serving everything from traditional Chinese dim sum to Vietnamese pho

BELOW, LEFT AND RIGHT: Illuminated dragons at the 2008 Chinese Lantern Festival; nighttime in Toronto's vibrant Chinatown. FACING PAGE: This sculpture along Spadina Avenue marks the entrance to Chinatown. Artist Millie Chen's mythical creatures, atop tall red poles, spell out "gateway" in Chinese characters.

to modern Asian fusion dishes. There are shops devoted only to tea or herbal medicines. Below street level, there are cocktail lounges and lively karaoke bars.

Chinese New Year celebrations always feature colourful live stage shows, martial arts demonstrations and lion dances, but the Toronto Chinatown BIA hosts its weekend Toronto Chinatown Festival in mid-August. This non-profit warm-weather event pays tribute to the Chinese culture and typically attracts more than 100,000 people. There are elaborate performances of the dragon dance and the lion dance, as well as traditional dancing and opera and traditional and modern Asian music. Local Asian artists present their modern approach to Asian art and craft. Multicultural street food vendors sell fresh, authentic dishes and treats from across Asia. And Kung Fu masters from the city's many different schools and disciplines demonstrate their skills alongside their students.

East Chinatown extends from the intersection of Broadview Avenue and Gerrard Street, and Markham and Mississauga each have their own Chinatown districts. In all, there are six Chinatown neighbourhoods in the GTA, but Old Chinatown is the place to start.

Things to See & Do

- Stroll the streets and take in the sounds and aromas.
- Try a new East Asian restaurant.
- Attend Chinese New Year celebrations.
- Take in the free performances at the Toronto Chinatown Festival.

Chinatown BIA
Unit D, 2nd Floor
287 Spadina Avenue
Toronto, ON M6T 2E6
416-260-9800
chinatownbia.com

27

CN TOWER
∼ Toronto

RIGHT: An outdoor Sky Terrace view of Lake Ontario. Experience the breeze at 342 metres (1,122 ft). FACING PAGE, TOP AND BOTTOM: The CN Tower easily dominates the Toronto waterfront; a photo of the tower taken from the Centre Island ferry.

Things to See & Do

- Ride the outdoor glass elevators to the LookOut.
- Venture onto the Glass Floor and look down.
- Dine in revolving restaurant 360.
- Experience EdgeWalk, the world's highest hands-free walkway.

CN Tower
301 Front Street West
Toronto, ON M5V 2T6
416-868-6937
cntower.ca

While Canada's largest city has no shortage of memorable architecture, both historic and modern, the CN Tower is arguably its most recognizable structure. The western hemisphere's tallest free-standing structure dominates the city's harbourfront skyline and attracts more than two million visitors a year.

As the number of skyscrapers in the city multiplied mid-century, radio and television signals were increasingly deflected during transmission. In a bold effort to solve the problem (and make headlines), the Canadian National Railway (CN) decided to erect the tallest telecommunications tower in history. Built between 1973 and 1976, the tower stands over 553 metres (1,815 ft) tall and in 1995 was declared one of the Seven Wonders of the Modern World by the American Society of Civil Engineers, joining such notable landmarks as the English Channel Tunnel, the Panama Canal and the Golden Gate Bridge. Today, the tower's microwave telecommunications receptors provide Torontonians with remarkably clear reception, among the best in North America.

The CN Tower is almost twice as tall as the Eiffel Tower. A 2,579-step staircase is housed in its interior, though most visitors prefer to take the 58-second ride to the LookOut level — at 346 metres (1,136 ft) — aboard one of six glass-fronted outdoor elevators. There, visitors find spectacular views of Toronto and Lake Ontario. The tower's two new panoramic floor-to-ceiling "Window Walls"

contain thermochromic film, which allows the glass to adjust its darkness based on sunlight and external temperature.

The Glass Floor is another of the tower's must-see attractions. Visitors can look through the transparent floor and see 342 metres (1,122 ft) below. This level also features the Outdoor SkyTerrace, where you can step outside and feel the breeze.

An elevator on the LookOut level climbs an additional 33 storeys through the core of the tower to the SkyPod, one of the world's highest public observation decks, which looks down on Ontario's capital city from a height of 447 metres (1,465 ft).

The tower's famous revolving restaurant, 360, offers constantly changing views at 351 metres (1,152 ft). And if you would like to walk on *top* of the restaurant, there's EdgeWalk, the tower's latest attraction. The world's highest hands-free walkway encircles the top of the tower's main pod. While harnessed to an overhead safety rail, participants walk in groups of six along the 1.5-metre-wide (5 ft) walkway at 356 metres (1,168 ft) above the ground, with nothing but air and breathtaking views beneath them.

Each fixture in the tower's microprocessor-controlled LED lighting scheme can produce 16.7 million colours. Since it was launched in 2007, the CN Tower has used themed colour changes to help raise awareness for hundreds of charities and special causes.

28

THE DISTILLERY HISTORIC DISTRICT

~ Toronto

In the late 1800s, the Gooderham & Worts waterfront distillery enterprise grew to become one of Canada's biggest business success stories. At its height, the company was responsible for half of the country's spirits production and was one of Toronto's largest employers. But company growth slowed as beer and wine became popular, and the Ontario Temperance Act of 1916 caused more turmoil. Gooderham & Worts sold the company in 1923, and distillery operations continued under subsequent owners until the early 1990s.

In the early 21st century, a visionary group of developers took this collection of run-down Victorian industrial buildings, some dating to the 1860s, and transformed them into more than just another signposted historic neighbourhood. The idea was to create a distinctly compelling destination within the city,

The Gooderham & Worts Limited sign welcomes visitors to The Distillery Historic District.

ABOVE LEFT: Tourists flock to the Distillery District in all seasons, including winter, to take in the atmosphere and visit gallerys, restaurants and pubs. ABOVE RIGHT: A giant spider sprawls over the cobblestones, dwarfing visitors.

a place where artists, artisans, entrepreneurs and restaurateurs would inspire one another as well as visitors to their establishments. The idea worked.

The 47 buildings known as the Gooderham & Worts Distillery were restored and repurposed, and the original wood, brick and stone was incorporated wherever possible. Hundreds of tradesmen and craftsmen found ways to blend those original structural elements with modern materials and green technologies. The resulting Distillery Historic District is an internationally acclaimed pedestrian-only village devoted to arts, culture, entertainment and one-of-a-kind commerce.

Located within easy walking distance from downtown, the Distillery District is a hub for artists, with numerous studios, studio shops and galleries. There are more than 70 ground-level cultural and retail establishments, as well as over 80 shops and boutiques specializing in handcrafted furniture, pottery, clothing, jewellery and more. The Distillery also features at least 16 cafes, restaurants, lounges and pubs, including the Mill Street Brewery's popular onsite brew pub.

Two tank houses from the old Gooderham & Worts operations are home to the Young Centre for the Performing Arts, which houses four studio spaces and four theatres and is jointly operated by the Soulpepper Theatre Company and the George Brown Theatre School.

The Distillery Historical District's inspired restorations have made it one of Toronto's top tourist attractions.

Things to See & Do

- Enjoy pedestrian-only boutique shopping.
- Watch artists at work.
- Relax with a pint at the Mill Street Brewery.
- Catch a theatre performance.

The Distillery
Historic District
9 Trinity Street
Suite 200
Toronto ON M5A 3C4
416-364-1177
thedistillerydistrict.com

A sprawling 161 hectares (399 acres), High Park is a gift to Toronto residents and visitors that is filled with recreational possibilities, from scenic walking and cycling trails, gardens, swimming and wading pools to two baseball diamonds, tennis courts, soccer fields and an outdoor ice rink in winter. There's even a chess house.

A third of the park remains in a natural state, with rare oak savannah ecology. Highparknature.org is a great online source for the many ways to explore the park's woodlands, wetlands, gardens, creeks and ponds. Park wildlife includes squirrels, chipmunks, groundhogs, rabbits, opossums, (mostly nocturnal) raccoons and skunks, as well as red fox, coyotes and white-tailed deer. Muskrat and beaver can be seen in Grenadier Pond and other ponds and wetlands, along with 150 bird species, 69 butterfly species and nine species of amphibians and reptiles.

More animals can be found at the popular High Park Zoo, established in

1893. The zoo's 11 paddocks are home to species from around the world, including bison, llamas, sheep, reindeer, highland cattle, wallabies, capybaras, peacocks and emus. The zoo is free and attracts more than 700,000 visitors each year. Children will also enjoy the four playgrounds, particularly the castle-like Jamie Bell Adventure Playground. Families can tour the park's extended reaches aboard the Trackless Trains.

In late April to early May, the park's groves of Japanese cherry trees bloom in spectacular fashion and invite memorable strolls. Another peaceful attraction is the High Park Labyrinth, located north of the café. Inscribed on a concrete circle formerly used for a picnic shelter, the labyrinth's circles encourage "walking meditation" and are a reminder of the cycles of nature.

On summer evenings, the Canadian Stage theatre company performs under the stars in the amphitheatre as part of Shakespeare in the Park, the longest-running outdoor theatre event in Canada.

The park's boundaries are Bloor Street West (north), Parkside Drive (east),

Things to See & Do

- Tour the gardens and wild areas aboard the Trackless Train.
- Visit the High Park Zoo.
- Attend Shakespeare in the Park.
- Discover the Jamie Bell Adventure Playground.

High Park
1873 Bloor Street West
Toronto, ON M6R 2Z3
416-338-0338
highparktoronto.com
highpark.org
highparknature.org

the Queensway (south) and Grenadier Pond (west). The land was left to the City of Toronto by its owner, architect and engineer John George Howard, and opened to the public in 1876. A temperate man, Howard stipulated that no alcohol was to be consumed in the park. High Park thus remains the last "dry" area in the city, as its various eateries continue to abide by their benefactor's wishes.

FACING PAGE, TOP: High Park's groves of Japanese cherry trees blossom fragrantly each spring. FACING PAGE, BOTTOM: High Park in autumn. ABOVE: A High Park picnic spot covered in winter snow. LEFT: An explosion of colour near one of High Park's several ponds.

30 HOCKEY HALL OF FAME
~ Toronto

Located in the former Bank of Montreal building at the corner of Yonge and Front streets, the Hockey Hall of Fame offers puck pilgrims 4,700 square metres (50,600 sq ft) of hockey nirvana, including the original 1892 Stanley Cup — or the "Dominion Hockey Challenge Cup," as it was known at the time of its introduction. It houses the world's largest collection of hockey memorabilia, from obscure collectibles to equipment and jerseys worn by legendary players in historic games.

This original version of the Cup, along with other National Hockey League trophies and rings, are displayed in the bank vault just off the Esso Great Hall. The Great Hall is home to the current Stanley Cup (the Presentation Cup) when it's not travelling. When it's on the road, a convincingly detailed replica holds its spot. The Great Hall is also where the annual Hall of Fame induction ceremony takes place, and portraits and biographical sketches of each Hall of Fame member are on display.

The NHL Zone is divided into exhibits highlighting the NHL Today (current teams and players), NHL Retro (every

ABOVE: When it's not on the road, the Stanley Cup makes its home in the Hockey Hall of Fame. RIGHT: The Hall of Fame commissioned this five-metre-long (17 ft) bronze sculpture from Oakville artist Edie Parker in 1993. The work, entitled *Our Game*, is located along Front Street, to the left of the hall's entrance.

ABOVE: The distinguished-looking home of the Hockey Hall of Fame is a former Bank of Montreal building. BELOW: A young fan considers the 2.7-metre-high (9 ft) statue of Ken Dryden, one of two that guard the entrance to the Hall of Fame. The other depicts Cyclone Taylor.

Things to See & Do

- Visit the Stanley Cup.
- Go one-on-one against Carey Price.
- Check out the old-school equipment.
- Watch *Stanley's Game Seven* in 3-D.

Hockey Hall of Fame
Brookfield Place
30 Yonge Street
Toronto, ON M5E 1X8
416-360-7735
hhof.com

team that ever played in the league), NHL Legends (memorable players and coaches) and NHL Milestones (rosters, records and dynasties). There is even an old Montreal Forum-era replica of the Montreal Canadiens' dressing room.

Interactive displays allow visitors to go one-on-one against life-sized animated versions of the league's greatest goalies and shooters and to call the play-by-play for some of hockey's greatest goal-scoring moments. Two theatres show the best of hockey on film, including the 3-D documentary *Stanley's Game Seven*.

Although the NHL takes centre stage at the Hall of Fame, there is also a Hometown Hockey section that celebrates grass-roots hockey throughout North America. The expanded World of Hockey Zone covers international leagues and players, including World and Olympic competition.

81

31

MASSEY HALL & ROY THOMSON HALL

∼ Toronto

The Corporation of Massey Hall and Roy Thomson Hall operates two of Canada's premier concert halls, which showcase the world's top performers. The two related halls also happen to have some of the best acoustics in the city — Massey Hall in its natural reverb, Roy Thomson Hall through state-of-the-art sound design.

Commissioned by agricultural-equipment magnate Hart Massey as a place for "substantial and comfortable" public meetings, conventions and entertainment, Massey Hall opened in 1894. The hall was designed to seat 3,500, but renovations in the 1940s reduced seating to 2,765. Its exterior architecture is Palladian, while its interior is considered Moorish Revival.

Notable early appearances include Winston Churchill (1900, 1901), Carrie Nation (1901), Enrico Caruso (1908), Luisa Tetrazzini (1912), the London Symphony Orchestra under Arthur Nikisch (1912) and an exhibition boxing match featuring Jack Dempsey (1919). There were silent films, regular boxing matches and visits by touring opera, ballet and theatre companies.

Massey Hall was the home of the Toronto Symphony Orchestra and the Toronto Mendelssohn Choir until 1982, when they moved to newly built Roy Thomson Hall. The world's finest orchestras have played the Massey stage. Oscar Peterson and a 13-year-old Glenn Gould made their Massey Hall debuts within weeks of each other in March 1946. Charlie Parker and Dizzy Gillespie performed here on May 15, 1953, backed by Bud Powell, Charles Mingus and Max Roach, in what many critics consider "the greatest jazz concert ever."

Night after night, the hall serves Torontonians' diverse tastes. (Successive nights in late November 1969 witnessed performances by the Prague Chamber Orchestra, Charlie Pride & Kitty Wells, and the Moody Blues.) Gordon Lightfoot, its most frequently appearing artist, called Massey Hall "the centre of my universe as a musician."

It has been designated a National Historic Site of Canada and a City of Toronto Heritage Site.

Roy Thomson Hall, in the downtown entertainment district, was known as "The New Massey Hall" during its design and construction phases. It acquired its official name in 1982, thanks to the family of Roy Thomson (first Lord Thomson of Fleet, founder of the Thomson publishing empire), who donated $4.5 million to complete the fundraising efforts for the new hall.

Designed by Canadian architects Arthur Erickson/Mathers & Haldenby, its distinctive curvilinear honeycombed glass canopy remains an eye-catching struc-

Things to See & Do

- Hear your favourite artist or band at Massey Hall.
- Discover there are no bad seats (except the ones behind support columns).
- Hear the Toronto Symphony in its home auditorium.
- Attend an acoustically amazing gala concert.

Massey Hall
178 Victoria Street
Toronto, ON M5B 1T7
416-872-4255
masseyhall.com

Roy Thomson Hall
60 Simcoe Street
Toronto, ON M5J 2H5
416-872-4255
roythomsonhall.com

ABOVE: Historic Massey Hall's three distinctive red entrance doors. This hall has seen it all, from Carrie Nation to Feist. LEFT: The view from the stage. Although Massey seats almost 3,000, the hall's sightlines and acoustics make each performance an intimate experience.

FACING PAGE: Designed by Canadian architects Arthur Erickson/Mathers & Haldenby, Roy Thomson Hall's curvilinear glass canopy makes it stand out among downtown's skyscrapers. LEFT: Night view of Roy Thomson Hall. BELOW LEFT: A view from the lobby. BELOW RIGHT: Roy Thomson Hall offers patrons many perspectives from which to enjoy a performance.

ture amid the city's skyscrapers. The hall's original sound panels were the work of acoustician Theodore J. Schultz of Bolt, Beranek & Newman Inc., New York.

Roy Thomson seats 2,630 guests and is long-term home to the Toronto Symphony Orchestra and Toronto Mendelssohn Choir. The centrepiece of the auditorium is a 5,207-pipe organ built by Gabriel Kney, with tonal assistance from Andrew Davis and Hugh McLean.

In 2000, the hall unveiled a $20-million plan to further improve the auditorium's acoustics. Twenty-three new bulkheads, built from thin layers of fibreboard and Canadian white maple, now line the upper chamber and bring the reflective surfaces nearer the audience, enhancing the sound's impact and clarity.

While Roy Thomson Hall is known for its world-class classical performances, over the years its programming has included festivals, royal galas, centennial celebrations, art shows and pop, rock, jazz and world music concerts. Landmark performances have included the 1999 Millennium Opera Gala, with Isabel Bayrakdarian, Russell Braun, Measha Brueggergosman, Tracy Dahl, Frances Ginzer, Ben Heppner, Richard Margison, Brett Polegato, Gino Quilico, Catherine Robbin, Michael Schade and Jean Stilwell; and the 2002 Golden Jubilee Gala for Queen Elizabeth II, with the Toronto Symphony, the Toronto Mendelssohn Choir, Ginette Reno, the Tragically Hip and the Oscar Peterson Quartet.

32

ROYAL ONTARIO MUSEUM
~ Toronto

The ROM's main entrance is contained in the 2007 "Crystal" on Bloor Street West (seen here), but in celebration of Canada's 150th anniversary in 2017, the museum also reopened its thoroughly renovated and enhanced Queen's Park entrance, now known as the Weston Entrance.

The Royal Ontario Museum (ROM) is the largest museum in Canada and among the largest in North America. Beyond its vast holdings — more than six million items and 40 separate galleries — the museum is also Canada's largest field-research institution, leading or participating in research and conservation around the globe.

But you'll be wowed even before you walk inside. Inspired by the ROM's gem and mineral collection, the museum's striking architectural facelift has been called the "Crystal" because of its crystalline shape. Designed by Studio Daniel Libeskind as part of the Renaissance ROM renovation and expansion project, the massive, up-thrust, angular exterior cladding on Bloor Street West is 25 percent glass and 75 percent brushed-aluminum. The museum's main entrance is contained in the Lee-Chin Crystal (so named because of philanthropist Michael Lee-Chin's extraordinary $30-million gift toward the project).

Opened in 1914, the ROM showcases art, culture and nature from around the globe and across the ages. Among the museum's notable collections are its minerals and meteorites; its Near Eastern, African and East Asian art; its many artifacts of European and Canadian history; and, of course, its dinosaurs — the world's largest collection of fossils from the Burgess Shale, with more than 150,000 specimens.

The ROM's collections and fields of research are divided into eight Centres of Discovery: Ancient Cultures, Biodiversity, Contemporary Culture, Canada, Earth & Space, Fossils & Evolution, Textiles & Fashion and World Art & Culture.

ROM Ancient Cultures covers such topics as our early human ancestors in China, technological innovations of Mesopotamia and the global economy of ancient Rome, examining ancient cultures to help us understand the diversity of human experience.

ROM Biodiversity includes all living things and their complex interactions — the interconnected web of living systems.

ROM Contemporary Culture engages today's leading creators and thinkers, the people who challenge us to look at our world in new ways.

ROM Canada looks at our nation's heritage: its

Indigenous cultures, then its English and French settlement, and later its mosaic of international immigration.

Some of the meteorites, rocks, precious minerals and gems in ROM Earth & Space date back more than 4.5 billion years, making it one of the finest museum collections on display anywhere.

The ROM Fossils & Evolution exhibit is based on the work of the museum's paleontologists. By discovering, preserving and studying fossils from around the world, we learn how life evolved over time, which may contribute to our understanding of climate change and biodiversity loss today.

ROM Textiles & Fashion looks at clothing and other textiles in use from prehistory to the present day, with rotating exhibits of weaving, needlework, printed and archaeological textiles, and silks.

ROM World Art & Culture is home to one of the world's most extensive and eclectic collections of art and other cultural and historical objects. The scale of

FACING PAGE: Mosiac patterns on the dome ceiling of the Royal Ontario Museum's historic Rotunda entrance. ABOVE: The Eaton Gallery of Rome contains the largest collection of Roman artifacts in Canada. LEFT TOP: The sculptural work found in the Matthews Family Court of Chinese Sculpture spans 1,500 years of Chinese history. LEFT MIDDLE: Specimens in the James and Louise Temerty Galleries of the Age of Dinosaurs represent life during the Jurassic and Cretaceous periods. LEFT BOTTOM: The Teck Suite of Galleries: Earth's Treasures features displays of meteorites, rocks, precious minerals and gems.

Things to See & Do

- Enter through the Lee-Chin Crystal.
- See the world's largest collection of fossils.
- Choose a different Centre of Discovery for each visit.
- Attend a talk, seminar or workshop.

Royal Ontario Museum
100 Queen's Park
Toronto, ON M5S 2C6
416-586-8000
rom.on.ca

the museum's collection is enormous, with tens of thousands of artifacts representing the entire sweep of human history.

Among the museum's other highlights is the Daphne Cockwell Gallery of Canada's First Peoples exhibit on Level 1. It contains more than 1,000 artifacts (rotated for preservation purposes) that provide a cultural context for Canada's First Peoples and which examine the economic and social forces that have influenced Native culture and art. On Level 2, the family-friendly Patrick and Barbara Keenan Family Gallery of Hands-on Biodiversity features mossy frogs, a shark jaw, snakeskin, a fox's den and other touchable specimens and interactive displays. The Sir Christopher Ondaatje South Asian Gallery on Level 3 considers more than 5,000 years of South Asian history through 350 intriguing objects, drawn from an evolving collection of over 7,000 artifacts.

Of course the ROM's featured exhibitions change on a regular basis and permanent collections rotate displays, so there's always something new and interesting. The museum also holds tours, talks, performances, workshops, courses, children's programs and patron events.

33 ST. LAWRENCE MARKET
～ Toronto

ABOVE: This massive 19th-century brick building in downtown Toronto is home to the city's largest market. FACING PAGE, CLOCKWISE FROM TOP: Built in 1850, the market was restored to its original appearance in 1967; farmers from across the province bring their freshest seasonal produce; the popular Future Bakery is among the market's more than 120 vendors.

Truly one of the world's great markets, St. Lawrence Market caters to neighbourhood residents, is a destination market for Torontonians from other parts of the city and is a popular downtown attraction for visitors and tourists. The food is fresh, the air is aromatic, and the banter is jovial.

Located in the heart of historic Old Toronto, the St. Lawrence Market Complex comprises three main buildings: the South Market, the North Market and St. Lawrence Hall.

The South Market's main and lower levels are home to more than 120 specialty vendors offering some of the city's best fruits and vegetables, meat, fish, grains and baked goods, and dairy products, as well as unique non-food items. Almost every culture's cuisine is properly represented here. The Market Gallery, an exhibition space for the City of Toronto's Cultural Services, is found on the second floor of the South Market.

The North Market is best known for its Saturday Farmers' Market, which has been held on this site (in a sequence of buildings) since 1803. Farmers from all over southern Ontario bring their freshest seasonal produce to market here. On Sundays, the North Market and surrounding plaza host over 80 antique dealers, who display their wide range of wares from early morning until 5 p.m. It's a great way to spend a rainy day. (At the time of writing, the North Market was being redeveloped, with a temporary structure at 125 The Esplanade serving as Saturday Farmers' Market and the Sunday Antique Market.)

Built in 1850 and restored to its original grandeur in 1967, St. Lawrence Hall houses retail businesses on the ground floor and City offices on the second floor. The third floor contains the Great Hall, an extremely popular rental space for weddings and other special events.

The Market also offers cooking classes, knife skills sessions, History Talk & Tea gatherings and other weekly and monthly events. In May, the St. Lawrence Market neighbourhood witnesses the Criterion Bike Race, with $20,000 in prizes, while in June, there's Woofstock, North America's "largest outdoor festival for dogs." Every August, BuskerFest takes over the streets for four days. ～

Things to See & Do

- Try a new food from one of more than 120 vendors.
- Spend Sunday at the Antique Market.
- Take a specialty cooking class.
- Attend Woofstock.

St. Lawrence Market
92–95 Front Street East
Toronto, ON M5E 1C3
416-392-7219
stlawrencemarket.com

34

TORONTO CARIBBEAN CARNIVAL PARADE

~ Toronto

The Toronto Caribbean Carnival is a three-week cultural celebration of Caribbean music, costume and cuisine. Its organizers claim it is "North America's largest cultural festival." It might be. It is big and lively and colourful and well attended. The 50th anniversary of the carnival raised things to a higher level in 2017.

Formerly known as Caribana, the Toronto Caribbean Carnival is held each summer in downtown Toronto and sees some two million visitors, with up to 1.3 million spectators for the festival's final parade, which traditionally coincides with the civic holiday in August. Work on next year's costumes begins soon after the previous year's celebrations, and in many cases, a full year is devoted to creating these lavish creations.

The festival was introduced to Canada by its many Caribbean immigrants. Much of the festival's music, such as steel pan, soca and calypso, originates in Trinidad and Tobago, Jamaica, Barbados, Grenada, St. Lucia, St. Vincent and Antigua.

Toronto's Official Carnival Launch ceremony gives the City of Toronto a taste of what's to come in the weeks leading up to the parade. Carnival Village

ABOVE: Smiling, costume-clad participants pose during the annual Carnival Parade, North America's largest Caribbean parade. RIGHT: Many participants work an entire year on costumes for this colourful event. FACING PAGE: Approximately two million visitors attend the Caribbean Carnival, now more than 50 years old.

offers a weeklong multidisciplinary program of activities whose goal is to promote the multicultural identity of the Regent Park community and its downtown-neighbours. The festival is a family-friendly, all-ages event involving workshops, concerts and street theatre.

Junior Caribbean Carnival King and Queen winners are announced at a Junior King and Queen Showcase and head up the Junior Carnival Parade and Family Day on the weekend before the grand parade.

The senior King and Queen Parade kicks off the Caribbean Carnival's final weekend, as it has every year since Carnival began. Leaders of Caribbean Mas bands don flamboyant costumes and perform for the parade judges and enthusiastic crowds. Male and female competitors are rated on the details of their costumes and how well they represent the parade's theme. At the end of the night, a King and Queen are crowned.

On the morning of the main parade, the Caribbean community hosts a smaller pre-dawn parade known as J'ouvert. In Caribbean Creole, this means "day opening." The J'ouvert parade is intensely rhythmic, with steelpan bands and improvised musical instruments. Both spectators and parade participants often cover themselves with mud, flour, baby powder or watercolour paints, in the tradition of Caribbean J'ouvert celebrations.

Finally, after months of preparation, the city welcomes the Caribbean Carnival Grande Parade, with masqueraders in wild, extravagant, colourful costumes. As they wind their way from Exhibition Place along Lake Shore Boulevard, the road becomes the stage. The Parade of Bands features countless costumed dancers (called "Mas players") dancing to live and recorded Caribbean music. Toronto comes alive with the rhythms of calypso, soca, salsa, zouk and reggae.

Things to See & Do

- Attend the Official Launch ceremony.
- Sample the food during Carnival festivities.
- Catch the flamboyant King and Queen Parade.
- Be there for the raucous Grande Parade.

Toronto Caribbean Carnival
19 Waterman Avenue #200
Toronto, ON M4B 1Y2
416-391-5608
carnival.to

35

TORONTO PRIDE FESTIVAL & PARADE

∼ Toronto

The annual Toronto Pride Festival is the largest and longest LGBTQ celebration in North America and ranks among the top 10 such events in the world. Pride festivities are among the City of Toronto's biggest attractions, with an estimated attendance of over a million people.

While June has been officially declared Pride Month in the city, the real party starts as the month goes on. Nuit Rose, a festival of queer art and performance, takes place mid-month, showcasing work by more than 50 local and international artists from diverse perspectives.

The 10-day Pride Festival commences the last week of June. Live musical performances, dance parties, films, theatre, comedy, readings, fashion shows, drag balls, galas — all manner of cultural events are presented by Torontonians and members of the international queer underground. The 22 city blocks that make up the festival site are closed to vehicular traffic.

The Gladstone Hotel's annual Pride exhibition of art, craft, fashion and literature takes over all four floors of the hotel with more than 50 vendors. Drag Queens Reading to Kids happens at Glad Day Bookshop, recently featuring drag performance artists Fay Slift and Miss Fluffy Souffle. Ripley's Aquarium holds its own Pride party, with neon-pink jellyfish providing the backdrop for rainbow mermaids and mermen.

It all culminates in the festival's final weekend. Friday features the Trans March, which is open to all trans and non-binary people, as well as their friends and allies. Saturday sees the Dyke March, a political demonstration open to all self-identified dykes. Cherry Bomb, the Official Dyke Day After-Party, is the city's biggest dance party for queer women and friends.

On the last Sunday of Pride Month, over 100,000 people turn out to witness the Pride Parade. More than 150 groups participate. There are LGBTQ people from every point on the sliding scale of gender, of every age and colour and shape and every philosophy and religion; there are glamorous drag queens and muscular rollerskaters and people in wheelchairs and enthusiastically pasty Canadian men in patriotic Speedos; there are naked people and dramatically clothed and coiffed people; there are gay children and parents and grandparents. Animal Rights Toronto, CAMH, CUPE, the Girl Guides, the Ontario Nurses' Association and the Toronto District School Board are there. The prime minister and premier of Ontario are there.

The parade lasts between three and four hours — it's amazing — and helps our province become a more inclusive place. ∼

Things to See & Do

- Attend Nuit Rose.
- Check out the Gladstone's Pride exhibition.
- Visit Ripley's Aquarium during the Pride Party.
- Get a good spot for the Pride Parade.

Pride Toronto
55 Berkeley Street
Toronto, ON
M5A 2W5
416-927-7433
pridetoronto.com

Pride Parade participants include people of diverse sexual and gender identities, from all ages, races and cultural backgrounds. It's a boisterous annual celebration of freedom, choice, support and inclusion.

36 THE WORD ON THE STREET
～ Toronto

The Word On The Street (WOTS) reading, writing and literacy festival is held each September in numerous cities across Canada, but it started in Toronto in 1990 (International Literacy Year) after the Book and Periodical Council decided that it was time for Canada's largest city — its "publishing capital" — to have a festival of the written word, as do many European publishing capitals.

The festival launched as the Toronto Book and Magazine Fair and more than 30,000 people attended. From the beginning, it had strong support not just from publishers and authors but from readers, the large-numbered and largely unseen participants in the publishing world.

In 1994, the incorporated Toronto Book and Magazine Fair Trust became The Word On The Street, a non-profit organization, and since then, regional festivals have developed from Vancouver to Halifax. The free festival holds hundreds of author events, presentations and workshops and gives readers (and writers) an opportunity to browse the marketplace. WOTS boasts the broad-

ABOVE: The Word On The Street festival offers plenty of activities, entertainment and books for children.
RIGHT: The festival is a family-friendly event, a chance for publishers and authors to connect with readers and to celebrate and cultivate a love of reading.

LEFT: Featured authors read their work to a crowd of listeners gathered in the Toronto Book Awards tent. BELOW: Word On The Street is Canada's largest annual book and magazine festival. It literally takes literacy to the streets.

est selection of Canadian books and magazines you'll find anywhere.

The mostly outdoor festival features author readings, panel discussions, workshops, information booths, authors' marketplace booths and all manner of reading-and-writing-related activities. WOTS' mandate is "to unite the country in a national, annual celebration of reading and writing and to highlight the importance of literacy in the lives of all Canadians."

Every year, The Word On The Street Toronto selects great Canadian reads to be featured in The Word On The Street's summer book club. Members have the opportunity to get ready for the festival early by digging into one of the literary treasures and meeting the author at the festival to discuss the book.

In 2017, WOTS ran its first writing contest, Writing DiverCity, a fiction contest for writers under 35, which aimed to highlight the diversity and range of emerging Canadian talent, encouraging participation from all backgrounds, orientations and identifications to show the variety and vibrancy of Canadian writers.

The Word On The Street Toronto has become Canada's largest annual book and magazine festival. As part of its commitment to supporting emerging artists, one quarter of the festival's exhibit space is available at cost to small presses, independent authors and writing associations. Literacy organizations are accommodated at no charge.

Lovers of spoken word can check out a youth and adult poetry slam at The Word On The Street, where The Guerrilla Poetry, Toronto Youth Poetry and Toronto Poetry Slam team all share their powerful messages in the open air.

The Book Bank operates a beautiful storefront in Regent Park, which welcomes schools and daycares, as well as families and their children to browse the shelves and choose a favourite book to take home to keep — for free.

Things to See & Do

- Discover your new favourite author.
- Take part in a book club discussion.
- Present your own book.
- Attend numerous author events for free.

The Word On The Street Toronto
67 Mowat Avenue
Suite 242
Toronto, ON M6K 3E3
416-504-7241
thewordonthestreet.ca/
toronto/festival

37

BALL'S FALLS & CATARACT TRAIL

～ Jordan/Ball's Falls

ABOVE: The historic chapel at Ball's Falls can seat up to 110 people and is a popular venue for weddings. FACING PAGE: The upper Ball's Falls cascade 11 metres (36 ft) down to the creek. During spring runoff, water flow increases dramatically.

Things to See & Do

- Explore both upper and lower falls.
- Visit Ball's Falls' historic village.
- Experience spectacular views of Twenty Valley.

Niagara Peninsula
  Conservation Authority
3292 Sixth Avenue
Lincoln, ON L0R 1S0
905-562-5235
npca.ca/conservation-
  areas/balls-falls

Located in the Niagara Region's scenic Twenty Valley, Ball's Falls Conservation Area offers inspiring natural beauty and a taste of 19th-century life.

The Cataract Trail follows the path of Twenty Mile Creek and features excellent views of the two falls that comprise Ball's Falls. The upper falls cascade 11 metres (36 ft), while the lower falls plunge a spectacular 25 metres (82 ft) over the Niagara Escarpment into a pool below. The falls change with the seasonal runoff and are at their most dramatic in the spring. Take time to appreciate the colourful layers of exposed rock surrounding the falls.

Birdwatchers will want to be on the lookout for as many as 50 species of migrant birds and 162 species of nesting birds. Many species of mammals and reptiles also make the Twenty Valley their home.

The Ball in Ball's Falls comes from the Ball family, United Empire Loyalists who settled here around 1807 on land granted as payment for their allegiance to the British during the American Revolution. The family built a gristmill and a sawmill at the lower falls and a woollen mill at the upper falls. Remnants of the Ball family sawmill can be seen along the trail.

The Niagara Peninsula Conservation Authority maintains the tiny hamlet in its mid-19th-century condition as a historic site, featuring the original Ball family home, a working flour mill, a lime kiln, a blacksmith's shop, a carriage shed and other period structures. The hamlet's historic church, with its rustic wooden interior and old-fashioned pump organ, can seat up to 110 people and is a popular venue for weddings.

You can extend your hike by taking the Forest Frolic Trail detour near the Cataract Trail's midpoint or by following links to the Twenty Valley Trail or the Bruce Trail. ～

38

BROCK'S MONUMENT & HISTORIC FORT GEORGE
～ Queenston Heights

Fifty-six metres (185 ft) high and the tallest of its kind in Canada, the monument to Major General Sir Isaac Brock is located on the site of the Battle of Queenston Heights. There, it guards the final resting place of Brock and his aide-de-camp, Lieutenant Colonel John Macdonell, who lost their lives repelling invading American forces during the first major engagement in the War of 1812.

A self-guided tour of the battlegrounds begins at the foot of the monument. Inside the monument itself are 235 stairs, which ascend to an area near the top that affords a magnificent view of the Niagara River, the surrounding landscape and beyond, to Lake Ontario.

Things to See & Do

- Discover over 250 years of Niagara history.
- Climb 235 stairs to the top of Brock's Monument.
- Fire a musket at old Fort George.

Brock's Monument
  National Historic Site
14184 Niagara River
Parkway
Queenston, ON
L0S 1P0
905-468-6621
friendsoffortgeorge.ca/
  brocks-monument

Fort George National
  Historic Site
51 Queen's Parade
Niagara-on-the-Lake
ON L0S 1J0
905-468-6614
pc.gc.ca/en/lhn-nhs/
  on/fortgeorge
905-468-6621
friendsoffortgeorge.ca/
  fort-george

In fact, this is the second monument built to honour Major General Brock. The first was badly damaged by the bomb of an alleged American sympathizer in 1840. Construction of the present monument commenced in 1853, and it was opened to the public in 1859. Today, costumed staff guide summer visitors, and a small museum reveals details about Brock's life.

Brock served at nearby Fort George, which is now a National Historic Site operated by Parks Canada and maintained much as it was during the War of 1812. Staff members wear period costumes and train summer students in the infantry tactics and firing drills of the 41st Regiment. Battle re-enactments have taken place on the fort's grounds since 1984, with the number of participants, both American and Canadian, growing from 300 to more than 1,800 during that time.

FACING PAGE: Redcoat-clad soldiers at Niagara-on-the-Lake raise their muskets in a re-enactment of a battle in the War of 1812. LEFT AND BELOW: The tallest monument in Canada marks the resting place of Sir Isaac Brock and his aide-de-camp.

39 CANADA'S LARGEST RIBFEST vs. NORTH AMERICA'S LARGEST VEGETARIAN FOOD FESTIVAL

～ Burlington/Toronto

You may have found yourself zooming along Highway 403 near Burlington, noticed an official government road sign announcing Home of Canada's Largest Ribfest, and wondered, as I did, "Who gets an official sign for their ribfest?"

The answer: The kind of people who can attract almost 200,000 guests to their long-weekend barbecue. The Rotary Club of Burlington Lakeshore has been holding this annual fundraising event for more than 20 years. To date, the service club has raised over $3 million for local community organizations and charities.

FACING PAGE: Canada's Largest Ribfest, in Burlington, features musical entertainment, an artisan fair, midway rides, a kids' zone and over 68,000 kilograms (150,000 lb) of award-winning ribs. The annual event has raised over $3 million for local organizations and charities. LEFT: Vegetarians enjoy outdoor grilling too. Hosted by the Toronto Vegetarian Association, Toronto's Veg Food Fest is held along the downtown waterfront at Harbourfront Centre in early September. BELOW: Marching with a smile at Toronto's Veggie Pride Parade.

The event has grown so popular that — well, it's "Canada's Largest Ribfest." Over 600 volunteers make sure this Labour Day weekend festival runs smoothly. The family fun includes plenty of musical entertainment, an artisan fair, midway rides, a kids' zone and over 68,000 kilograms (150,000 lb) of award-winning ribs. Nineteen "ribber" teams from across North America — with names such as Bone Daddy,

Things to See & Do

- Sample the ribs from 19 top barbecue rigs.
- Head to the midway and catch the musical performances.
- Experience the newest in vegetarian cuisine.
- Celebrate Ontario's dietary diversity.

Spencer Smith Park
1400 Lakeshore Road
Burlington, ON
L7M 4R1
canadaslargestribfest.
com

Rotary Club of
Burlington Lakeshore
905-332-3513

Toronto Vegetarian
Association
17 Baldwin Street
2nd floor
Toronto, ON M5T 1L1
416-544-9800
veg.ca/events/
vegfoodfest

Hawgs Gone Wild, Sticky Fingers and Dinosaur BBQ Pit — set up their travelling rigs in Spencer Smith Park and compete for Best Ribs, Best Sauce and Best Pig Rig titles.

And while you might guess that this four-day carnivore's picnic would create a tsunami of trash, the Rotary Club of Burlington Lakeshore is dedicated to making sure their event produces only biodegradable waste and therefore relies on 100-percent recyclable materials. As a result, Canada's Largest Ribfest is a seven-time winner of Festivals & Events Ontario's "Best Greening" award.

At the other end of the dietary continuum, there's Toronto's Veg Food Fest, held annually along the downtown waterfront at Harbourfront Centre in early September. Hosted by the Toronto Vegetarian Association, it began as a 500-person event in 1985 and has since grown into the leading event of its kind in North America and one of the largest vegetarian festivals in the world.

Veg Food Fest attracts more than 40,000 visitors and over 130 exhibitors. Weekend events include live cooking demonstrations, workshops, films and musical performances. Canadian and international chefs create delicious vegetarian and vegan dishes, and free samples abound.

A marketplace features vendors focused on the future of the vegetarian lifestyle, and new products, cookbooks and even entire businesses are launched over the course of the weekend. Veg Food Fest is free to the public.

40

CANADA'S WONDERLAND
～ Vaughan

Ontario is home to Canada's largest amusement and water park. Located on 134 hectares (330 acres) in suburban Vaughan, just north of Toronto, Canada's Wonderland is open daily from May through September, with weekend openings in late April, October and early November. The park's annual Halloween Haunt is almost a rite of passage for Greater Toronto Area teenagers.

Canada's Wonderland features some 70 rides (roller coasters, thrill rides, family rides and kids' rides), as well as a vast water park known as Splash Works, which takes up eight hectares (20 acres). With 16 roller coasters, Wonderland is ranked second in the world by number of coasters, tying with Cedar Point in Sandusky, Ohio, which bills itself as "The Roller Coaster Capital of the World." (Six Flags Magic Mountain in Santa Clarita, California, has 19 coasters.)

The Leviathan, ascending 93 metres (306 ft), is the tallest ride in the park. Riders drop from peak height on an 80-degree angle at speeds reaching 148 kilometres per hour (92 mph). The Behemoth rises 70 metres (230 ft) before sending riders downhill at a 75-degree angle, with speeds reaching 125 kilometres an hour (78 mph). The Behemoth's trains take riders along 1,606 metres (5,318 ft) of track, over four massive hills, around a 180-degree hairpin turn and through two helixes. Everyone has their favourite roller coaster, and often they aren't the highest or the fastest. Be sure to try Dragon Fire, Backlot Stunt Coaster, Flight Deck, Vortex, The Bat and Mighty Canadian Minebuster.

New to Wonderland's thrill rides is Soaring Timbers. Two rotating gondolas with room for 38 riders turn through a 360-degree cycle while the gondolas flip independently on a centre axis. Riders spin and flip in arcs that reach heights of 20 metres (66 ft). Drop Tower plummets 70 metres (230 ft) at a speed of five metres per second (16 fps). Night Mares spins from horizontal to vertical position. Sledge Hammer sends eight-person gondolas through hair-raising jumps and free falls. And SlingShot riders are launched up to 90 metres (295 ft) over Action Zone, where they have a face-to-face encounter with riders on the neighbouring 92-metre (301 ft) WindSeeker.

After the rides, Splash Works water park may help restore some of your cool. The popular new Muskoka Plunge is an 18-metre-high (60 ft) waterslide complex with four "trap-door" speed slides. Nearby Black Hole is a four-storey speed slide that sends tube riders through a winding black pipeline before emptying them back into daylight and clear water.

Splash Works offers kiddie slides, kiddie pools, the Pumphouse Playground and Splash Island Sprayground for younger visitors. The younger crowd will also enjoy the many possibilities found in KidZville and Planet Snoopy, with at least two-dozen family-friendly rides, slides and other activities. ～

Things to See & Do

- Ride up to 16 different rollercoasters.
- Plunge earthward aboard the Drop Tower.
- Shoot skyward aboard the SlingShot.
- Cool down at the many Splash Works attractions.

Canada's Wonderland
1 Canada's
 Wonderland Drive
Vaughan, ON L6A 1S6
905-832-8131
canadaswonderland.
 com

CLOCKWISE FROM TOP: Wonderland's Wonder Mountain with 18-metre (60 ft) Victoria Falls; the castle entrance to the park's Middle Ages-themed Medieval Faire; Canada's largest amusement park features more than 70 different rides, including 16 roller coasters.

41

CANADIAN WARPLANE HERITAGE MUSEUM
∼ Hamilton/Mount Hope

The Canadian Warplane Heritage Museum is not just about warplanes. Founded in 1972, it is a privately owned, non-profit aviation museum whose mandate is to acquire, preserve and maintain a complete collection of aircraft flown by Canadians and the Canadian military from the beginning of the Second World War to the present.

The museum is located at the John C. Munro Hamilton International Airport and features propeller-driven trainers, a flying boat, transport planes, spotters, fighters, bombers, a Bell helicopter and the cockpit of a Boeing 727. It currently houses almost 50 aircraft, many in flying condition. These are used in airshows, film productions and for scheduled private flights. Museum members can pay a fee upgrade to enjoy a flight in many of these airworthy historic planes.

Among the airworthy aircraft are a 1939 Douglas DC-3 Dakota, a 1941 de Havilland DH.82C Tiger Moth, a 1942 Boeing PT-17 Stearman, a 1943 Fairchild Cornell Mk. II, a 1944 Consolidated Canso PBY-5A flying boat, a 1945 Avro Lancaster Mk. X, a 1945 North American B-25J Mitchell Mk. III, a 1946 Beechcraft Expeditor, a 1950 Noorduyn Norseman Mk. V, a 1951 North American Harvard Mk. IV and a 1956 de Havilland Canada DHC-1B-2-S5 Chipmunk.

BELOW, LEFT TO RIGHT: The museum's twin-engined 1941 Cessna Crane Mk.1 trainer on display; located at the John C. Munro Hamilton International Airport, the museum houses almost 50 diverse aircraft; the revolutionary Lockheed CF-104D Starfighter set world altitude and speed records between 1958 and 1963.

Fighters on display include a 1958 Avro Canada CF-100 Canuck, a 1960 de Havilland DH.100 Vampire FB.6, a 1970 Northrop CF-5A Freedom Fighter and a Lockheed CF-104 Starfighter. The museum is also restoring several Second World War and Cold War aircraft. Museum curators also seek to preserve artifacts, books, periodicals and manuals relating to their aircraft.

The Avro Lancaster flown by the museum is one of only two airworthy Lancasters in the world. Named the Mynarski Memorial Lancaster, in honour of P/O Andrew Charles "Andy" Mynarski, VC, it is painted in the markings of his aircraft. In the summer of 2014, the museum flew "Mynarski's Lanc" to England, where it joined the RAF Battle of Britain Memorial Flight's Lancaster for a two-month tour of England, Scotland, Northern Ireland and the Channel Islands. The tour was witnessed by millions and was filmed for the documentary DVD *Reunion of Giants*.

In the Kid Zone, young would-be pilots can pick their simulated aircraft — a Chipmunk trainer, the Lancaster bomber, the supersonic CF-101 Voodoo jet — and take off from Hamilton International Airport for a smooth, easy flight or one full of loops and rolls.

Even experienced pilots enjoy the Air Combat Zone F-18 Hornet flight simulators. When you climb aboard an Air Combat Zone simulator and settle into the ejection seat, you'll be amazed at the realistic cockpit — live instrumentation, head-up display, replica HOTAS throttle and stick, and the big-screen view of the world outside. The Air Combat Zone experience includes a pre-flight briefing to give you the instruction you need to survive in your cyber battle. You also receive mission support from staff in the control tower. It's "as close as you can get to the real thing without joining the Air Force!"

Things to See & Do

- Discover Canadian aircraft history up close and hands-on.
- Check out decades of fighter aircraft development.
- See one of the world's two airworthy Lancaster bombers.
- Fly an F-18 Hornet in simulated battle in the Air Combat Zone.

Canadian Warplane Heritage Museum
9280 Airport Road
Mount Hope, ON
L0R 1W0
905-679-4183
1-877-347-3359
warplane.com

42

CITY OF WATERFALLS
∽ Hamilton

Hamilton has long fought a public image problem. Most Canadians think of Hamilton as a pollution-spewing industrial port city. Much has changed in recent times due to the decline of domestic manufacturing and a heightened civic awareness of things environmental, but the truth is, Hamilton has always possessed abundant natural beauty, and influential citizens and politicians have been working for decades to expand its parks and green space.

Goodbye, "Steeltown." Hello, "Waterfall Capital of the World." The Hamilton region is home to more than 100 waterfalls and cascades, the highest number of any urban area its size. Many of these waterfalls are found along the Niagara

FACING PAGE: The Spencer Trail follows picturesque Webster Falls in this colourful shot of autumn in the Hamilton region. BELOW: This is Tew's Falls, a large ribbon waterfall at Spencer Gorge/Webster's Falls Conservation Area.

Things to See & Do

- Visit a new waterfall each month.
- Pick and share favourites.
- Compare water flow in spring and autumn.
- Join the 22,000 plus Facebook members.

Hamilton Conservaton Authority
Main Administrative Office - Woodend
838 Mineral Springs Road
Ancaster, ON L9G 4X1
905-525-2181
conservationhamilton.ca
cityofwaterfalls.ca

Escarpment and the Bruce Trail and are easily accessible from groomed trails and viewing areas.

The website cityofwaterfalls.ca maintains a complete list of greater and lesser falls, with links to histories, descriptions and directions, along with a number of photographs. Among members' recommendations are Albion Falls and Webster's Falls (most popular), but there are also Baby Webster's Falls, Billy Green Falls, Borer's Falls, Chedoke Falls, Darnley Cascade, Devil's Punchbowl, Felker's Falls, Great Falls, Hermitage Cascade, Sherman Falls and Tiffany Falls. The City of Waterfalls team conducts guided waterfalls walks, which are announced on their Facebook page: Hamilton–Waterfall Capital of the World!

The Hamilton section of the Niagara Escarpment, which locals call "The Mountain," rises 100 metres (330 ft) in many locations, and it is from atop this wall of limestone, sandstone and shale that so many creeks and streams plunge to enter pools and waterways, many of which feed Hamilton Harbour.

Of course, all this water makes for lush vegetation, diverse animal populations and a focus on environmental tourism not previously associated with Hamilton's other nickname, "The Hammer." To that end, the Hamilton Conservation Authority manages more than 4,500 hectares (11,100 acres) within the city's current boundaries, and the City of Hamilton maintains 1,077 hectares (2,661 acres) of parkland at 310 locations.

"Hike Hamilton!" It has a nice ring to it. ⟋

Albion Falls is one of the largest and least disturbed cascades in the region. Panoramic views of the waterfall and its gorge are available from the higher ground west of the falls.

43

COBOURG BEACH &
SANDCASTLE FESTIVAL
∼ Cobourg

An artist adds stonework and lettering to her dragon sculpture at the Cobourg Sand Castle Festival, held annually on Cobourg Beach. Teams and individuals, professional and amateur, compete in front of as many as 10,000 spectators.

I t's just a beach, but it's one of the best beaches in the province. Sometimes all you want to do is relax and experience sun, sand and water, and Cobourg is an accessible distance from most population centres in southern Ontario — 110 kilometres (68 mi) east of Toronto, 145 kilometres (90 mi) west of Kingston.

Long known for its deep, white sand, its boardwalk and its panoramic views of Lake Ontario, Cobourg Beach was a popular destination for wealthy American tourists from 1905 to 1950, when regular car-ferry services connected Cobourg and Rochester, New York. Many built summer homes here and participated in local yacht races and pavilion dances. Almost 70 years later, the Cobourg Yacht Club still hosts events, and the Concert Band of Cobourg gives free performances

The Victoria Park entrance to Cobourg Beach. Free concerts and other events take place in Victoria Park all summer.

from Victoria Park's 1934 bandshell on Tuesday nights during the summer.

Cobourg Beach prides itself on being family-friendly. Children (and parents) will appreciate the splash pads, play equipment and climbing structures. And lifeguards keep watch over the clean, shallow waters during prime swimming hours. For older or physically challenged visitors, there is an accessibility mat that runs across the beach from the gazebo to the water's edge, allowing people using wheelchairs or walkers to reach the shoreline. The mat is great for strollers, as well.

Kayaks, canoes and paddleboards are available for rent, with options for individual or group lessons. There are even floating yoga classes.

Victoria Park, a park adjacent to the beach that encompasses nine hectares (22 acres), provides shade and food options. Operated by The Market & Smor, the beach canteen brings its fresh food right to the water's edge, with salads and sandwiches made from organic ingredients, bubble teas, coffees, smoothies and desserts. The Freakin Rican Food Truck next to the canteen serves inspired tacos and chorizo, as well as fried pickles and mozzarella sticks. The Hot Diggety Dog stand beside the campground sells dogs and more. And, of course, ice cream is always at hand (even vegan ice cream). Cobourg's historic downtown is located just a block north of the beach and is home to numerous restaurants, if you seek something more formal.

Free rock, pop, blues and country concerts and other events take place in Victoria Park throughout the summer.

An annual beach highlight is the Cobourg Sandcastle Festival, held in late July or early August. Eight North American master sculptors or teams vie for the best creation, while as many as 36 amateurs and teams try their luck. The competition draws crowds of up to 10,000. After the awards presentation, the day ends with a movie on the beach and fireworks over the pier.

Things to See & Do

- Dig your feet into the warm, white sand.
- Swim in the clear, shallow, lifeguard-patrolled water.
- Enjoy a free concert at Victoria Park's 1934 bandshell.
- Attend the Cobourg Sandcastle Festival.

Cobourg Tourism
750 D'Arcy Street
Cobourg, ON K9A 0G1
1-888-262-6874
cobourgtourism.ca

44

HALTON COUNTY RADIAL RAILWAY MUSEUM
∼ Milton

A close-up look at vintage emergency streetcar handles. At the Halton County Radial Railway Museum, visitors can see at least 20 streetcars dating from 1901 to 1951.

Owned and operated by the non-profit Ontario Electric Railway Historical Association (OERHA), the Halton County Radial Railway Museum is Ontario's first and largest electric railway museum. The full-sized, fully operational electric railway features historic electric railcars that run on two kilometres (1.2 mi) of scenic track.

The Halton County Radial Railway and the OERHA were formed in 1953 by a group of enthusiasts seeking to save Toronto Transit Commission (TTC) streetcar 1326 from the scrapyard. The TTC's donation of this streetcar led the group to expand their dream. Eventually, the volunteers acquired land that had once been part of the Toronto Suburban Railway in Nassagaweya Township, and more street and radial cars were rescued. The museum's grand opening took place in 1972.

Located between the villages of Rockwood and Campbellville, the museum is open to the public and offers rides on many of its vehicles. Located along part of the Toronto Suburban Railway's former right-of-way, the museum's tracks conform to the TTC's gauge (wider than standard gauge), so vehicles from other systems must be altered, and cars intended for third-rail power must be reconfigured for use with an overhead wire.

The Radial Railway is a working museum focused primarily on the history of the Toronto Transit Commission and its predecessor, the TTC, with a collection that includes Presidents' Conference Committee and Peter Witt cars, earlier streetcars, Gloucester series and Montreal-built subway cars, as well as other historic railway vehicles, trolleybuses and buses. Visitors can see at least 20 streetcars dating from 1901 to 1951. Highlights include two beautiful early 1920s Peter Witt cars built by Canadian Car & Foundry, as well as a half dozen Interurban & Suburban cars, most from the 1910s.

The museum offers several special holiday events, but generally speaking, it is open weekends and holidays during May and June and September and October, and every day in July and August. The first ride leaves at 11 a.m., and the last ride leaves 30 minutes before closing.

From the start, the museum's mandate was to inform, educate and inspire the public about the electric railway history of Ontario and Canada. In addition to its impressive collection of historic streetcars, radial cars and work cars, the museum maintains an archive of photographs, memorabilia and other materials. An Ontario Historical Plaque commemorates the Halton County Radial Railway Museum's role in Ontario's heritage preservation. ∼

Things to See & Do

- Take a ride on a restored 1920s streetcar.
- Learn about the evolution of the TTC and its streetcars.
- Experience a seasonal Christmas on the Rails.
- Find out which cars were used in Hollywood films.

Halton County
  Radial Railway
13629 Guelph Line
Milton, ON L9T 5A2
519-856-9802
hcry.org

CLOCKWISE FROM TOP: Leather seating in a 1920s vintage Peter Witt streetcar once operated by the Toronto Transit Commission; a vintage TTC subway sign; this 1923 TTC car 2894 was the last car to operate on the Dupont route in 1963.

45

HALTON HIGH POINTS
~ Mount Nemo, Rattlesnake Point, Kelso, Crawford Lake & Hilton Falls

Halton is Escarpment country, and despite the region's population density, the nearby cliffs offer urban dwellers plenty of ways to escape into nature.

Located north of Burlington on Guelph Line, Mount Nemo Conservation Area boasts two loop trails, about 2.5 kilometres (1.6 mi) each, which present some of the Escarpment's most magnificent views. In summertime, visitors can watch hawks and turkey vultures riding the thermals at eye level. Rock climbers will appreciate Mount Nemo's more than 200 climbing routes. Climb to the top for a rewarding lookout. Numerous cave systems run through the cliff face, making spelunking another popular activity.

Rattlesnake Point Conservation Area — named for the way the glaciers cut through the rock, not for the Massasauga rattlesnake — is one of the most popular rock-climbing destinations in southern Ontario. Three designated sites feature more than 235 routes. To protect the area's stunted ancient cedars, there is a ban on slinging trees, but the limestone cliffs are fitted with bolts for top-rope anchors. The park's 12.7 kilometres (8 mi) of cliff-edge and forest trails connect

RIGHT: Crawford Lake, near Campbellville, is one of only a few meromictic lakes (lakes whose layers do not intermix) in Canada. FACING PAGE: Rattlesnake Point's cliffs, seen here in autumn foliage, feature more than 235 climbing routes.

Things to See & Do

- Take in the Escarpment's best views at Mount Nemo.
- Try a few of the 235 rock-climbing sites at Rattlesnake Point.
- Visit the reconstructed 15th-century Iroquoian village at Crawford Lake.
- Sit beside the springtime roar of Hilton Falls.

Conservation Halton
2596 Britannia Road West
Burlington, ON
L7P 0G3
905-336-1158
conservationhalton.ca

with the Bruce Trail and Crawford Lake. The 7.2-kilometre (4.5 mi) Nassagaweya Trail hike can take about an hour or more, but there are many places along the way where hikers can pause and enjoy the view.

Across its 397 hectares (981 acres), the Kelso Conservation Area features 16 kilometres (10 mi)of marked trails along the Escarpment, with frequent lookout points and a boardwalk. The park also contains Lake Kelso, built for flood control of Sixteen Mile Creek. The lake has a sandy beach and is perfect for a cool-down swim in summer.

Crawford Lake Conservation Area, near Campbellville, has 19 kilometres (12 mi) of trails with connections to the Bruce Trail. A boardwalk circles the lake, protecting the fragile ferns and mosses underfoot. The trail is decorated with whimsical sculptures and benches. A secondary trail leads to the Escarpment, and another connects to nearby Rattlesnake Point Conservation Area. Archaeological evidence suggests that the site was once inhabited by the Wendat (Huron), affiliated with the Neutral Confederacy, and a reconstructed 15th-century Iroquoian village has been built in the park. The village includes three longhouses and a palisade and offers interpretive details of Iroquoian life and culture.

Also located near Campbellville, the Hilton Falls Conservation Area has 16 kilometres (10 mi) of hiking trails, mill ruins, a reservoir and a 10-metre (33 ft) waterfall that plunges from Sixteen Mile Creek into a cedar-lined gorge.

46 HIKING HEADWATERS COUNTRY
~ Erin, Caledon & Dufferin County

Ontario's Headwaters region derives its name from being the source of four major river systems: the Nottawasaga, the Credit, the Humber and the Grand. The massive watershed, some 253,400 hectares (626,165 acres), is home to numerous provincial parks and conservation areas, which contain some of southern Ontario's best — and most accessible — hiking opportunities. Located at the headwaters of the Grand River, Luther Marsh Wildlife

Management Area is one of southern Ontario's larger natural areas, with 5,900 hectares (14,580 acres) of forests, fields, wetlands and lakes, including Luther Lake. Both the East Launch Trail and North Launch Trail afford visitors plenty of chances for wildlife viewing.

The Boyne River flows east through the Orangeville and Singhampton moraines. Boyne Valley Provincial Park is found about 20 kilometres (12.4 mi) north of Orangeville. Its section of Bruce Trail, in the northern part of the park, provides an excellent lookout. The 8.4-kilometre (5.2 mi) Boyne Valley Side Loop Trail Boyne, located near Mulmur, is a great forest hike.

Located 14 kilometres (8.7 mi) northeast of Orangeville and four kilometres (2.5 mi) east of Mono Centre, Mono Cliffs Provincial Park is a Natural Environment-class park that is part of the Niagara Escarpment Parks System and the Niagara Escarpment Biosphere Reserve. With some 450 plant species found across its 750 hectares (1,853 acres), the trails are especially spectacular in the fall. The Bruce Trail passes through the park, and there are several interconnecting marked trails.

At 378 hectares (934 acres), the Hockley Valley Provincial Nature Reserve includes forested moraines, open meadows, swamp, bottomland and forest, with excellent views from the Niagara Escarpment. The Hockley River cuts its way through a gorge in the Escarpment. Several scenic loop trails extend from the Bruce Trail section that runs through the reserve.

Island Lake Conservation Area protects the headwaters of the Credit and Nottawasaga rivers. The area's 332 hectares (820 acres) of lakes, wetlands, forests and meadows play an important ecological role. The Vicki Barron Lakeside Trail, an 8.3-kilometre (5.2 mi) loop, allows you to see the park's full diversity.

Albion Hills Conservation Area offers trails for all skill levels. The northwest end of the Humber Valley Heritage Trail is located here. That trail runs 15 kilometres (9.3 mi) north from Bolton to connect with the Bruce Trail in Albion Hills. It begins at the headwaters of the Humber

FACING PAGE: Cannings Falls, on the Nottawasaga River near Hockley Valley Provincial Nature Reserve. BELOW: Springtime in Mono Cliffs Provincial Park. More than 450 plant species can be found along the park's trails.

FACING PAGE: An autumn walk through Mono Cliffs Provincial Park, near Orangeville. ABOVE: Hiking the hills of Forks of the Credit Provincial Park.

Things to See & Do

- Visit the headwaters of four major Ontario rivers.
- Explore the wetland habitat of Luther Marsh.
- Hike or bike the Caledon rail trail.
- Climb the 10,000-year-old hills of the Cataract Falls Trail.

Headwaters Tourism
246372 Hockley Road
Mono, ON
L9W 6K4
519-942-0314
1-800-332-9744
headwaters.ca

River, near Palgrave, and follows the Humber River Valley south, revealing scenic vistas en route.

The Caledon area boasts over 260 kilometres (162 mi) of accessible trails. The Town purchased a section of abandoned railway in 1989 and has created a multi-use rail trail that crosses the Humber and Credit rivers, the Oak Ridges Moraine and the Niagara Escarpment.

The Cataract Falls Trail in Forks of the Credit Provincial Park climbs steep hills that are remnants of gravel deposits (glacial till) left by glaciers when they melted more than 10,000 years ago.

Perhaps the most surprising landscape in the region belongs to the Cheltenham Badlands, a geological wonder now owned by the Ontario Heritage Trust and managed by a group that includes the Bruce Trail Conservancy. These red waves of exposed rock were at the bottom of an inland sea over 400 million years ago. While the sensitive natural area is temporarily closed to visitors to protect it from further damage, the Ontario Heritage Trust is undertaking a project to improve access, upgrade the trails and introduce new interpretive technology.

47

McMICHAEL CANADIAN ART COLLECTION
～ Kleinburg

Although Modernist in its design, the McMichael Canadian Art Collection building reflects the rugged aspects of the Ontario wilderness — hand-hewn square-timber logs and colourfully assembled fieldstone, with floor-to-ceiling windows that overlook the Humber River Valley. The McMichael facility houses 13 exhibition galleries focused entirely on Canadian art and the Indigenous art of our country, both historical and contemporary. It's the only collection of its kind in Canada.

Robert and Signe McMichael started their collection in 1955 after purchasing land in the village of Kleinburg. Inspired by their natural surroundings, the McMichaels began collecting work by Tom Thomson, the Group of Seven and

CLOCKWISE FROM TOP LEFT: The entrance sign to the McMichael; the gallery's main structure is made from salvaged hand-hewn pioneer logs and fieldstone masonry; the McMichael Canadian Art Collection stands alone as the only public fine-art gallery to focus on Canadian art and Indigenous art, both historical and contemporary.

ABOVE, LEFT TO RIGHT: Tom Thomson (1877–1917), *In Algonquin Park*, 1914, oil on canvas, gift of founders Robert and Signe McMichael in memory of Norman and Evelyn McMichael, 1966.16.76; Tom Thomson (1877–1917), *Woodland Waterfall*, 1916–1917, oil on canvas, purchase 1977 with funds donated by The W. Garfield Weston Foundation, 1977.48; Lawren S. Harris (1885–1970), *Icebergs, Davis Strait*, 1930, gift of Mr. and Mrs. H. Spencer Clark, 1971.17. All artworks courtesy of the McMichael Canadian Art Collection.

their contemporaries. By 1965, when they donated their home, art and land to the Province of Ontario, their collection comprised 194 artworks.

Today, the permanent collection holds more than 6,400 works by Thomson; the original Group of Seven (Franklin Carmichael, Frank Johnston, Lawren Harris, A.Y. Jackson, Arthur Lismer, J.E.H. MacDonald and F.H. Varley); later members A. J. Casson, Edwin Holgate and L. L. FitzGerald; Emily Carr, Clarence Gagnon and many other contemporaries; as well as important First Nations, Métis and Inuit artists.

The McMichael continues to explore trends and developments in Indigenous art and regularly acquires and exhibits work by new and noteworthy Indigenous artists. It also collects and exhibits a diverse range of paintings, prints, drawings and sculptures by contemporary Inuit artists in both the permanent collection and in special exhibitions. In addition, the McMichael is the gallery of record for the Cape Dorset Archive, and more than 100,000 drawings, prints and sculptures are on long-term loan from the West Baffin Eskimo Co-operative, based in Cape Dorset, Nunavut.

Each year, numerous exhibitions are curated from the permanent collection and from other major institutions and private collections. The McMichael offers art classes, workshops, talks and concerts for adults, as well as Saturday, March Break and summer events for children.

Beyond the galleries are 100 acres of forest. A network of paths and hiking trails run through natural stands of maple, oak and pine that were planted by the McMichaels to echo a northern forest. Here, visitors can explore the Ivan Eyre Sculpture Garden, a series of installations and outdoor sculptures, the Tom Thomson Shack, which was moved from its original location in the Rosedale ravine and reconstructed on the grounds of the McMichael, as well as the Artists' Cemetery, where six members of the Group of Seven are buried, along with gallery founders Robert and Signe McMichael.

Things to See & Do

- Discover the Group of Seven in a northern forest setting.
- See exhibits of contemporary First Nations, Métis and Inuit artists.
- Take an art class.
- Visit the Thomson Shack, Artists' Cemetery and Interpretive Trail.

McMichael Canadian Art Collection
10365 Islington Avenue
Kleinburg, ON L0J 1C0
905-893-1121
1-888-213-1121
mcmichael.com

48

NIAGARA-ON-THE-LAKE HISTORIC DISTRICT & THE SHAW FESTIVAL

~ Niagara-on-the-Lake

N iagara-on-the-Lake's perfectly maintained historic district, often called the Old Town, extends 25 city blocks and includes more than 90 residences, businesses, churches and government buildings, all constructed between 1815 and 1859 in the architectural style known as British Classical. The Old Town also includes Simcoe Park and two early 19th-century cemeteries. The citation that accompanied its 2003 designation as a National Historic Site of Canada describes it as possessing "the best collection of buildings in Canada from the period following the War of 1812."

The town was established in 1779 as a supply depot for British Loyalist forces. By the end of the 18th century, it had developed into a major military and cultural centre and served briefly as the capital of Upper Canada. Shipping and shipbuilding dominated local commerce between 1831 and 1859.

Niagara-on-the-Lake residents were among the first citizen coalitions in Canada to make a commitment to their architectural heritage. The Niagara Historical Society was established in 1896. Members collected artifacts, documents and published local histories. This foresight enabled many 20th-century residents to restore private properties to their authentic 19th-century appearance. Niagara-on-the-Lake was also one of the first Ontario municipalities to appoint a Local Architectural Conservation Advisory Committee.

Visitors strolling the Old Town will notice that the streets here are wide,

BELOW LEFT: Niagara-on-the-Lake's historic district extends 25 city blocks and includes more than 90 residences, businesses, churches and government buildings constructed between 1815 and 1859. BELOW RIGHT: The Royal George Theatre, 85 Queen Street, was built as a vaudeville house to entertain troops stationed in Niagara-on-the-Lake during the First World War. Inside, the Royal George is all Edwardian gilt mouldings, red walls and golden lions.

Niagara-on-the-Lake's Queen Street is equally charming on a snowy late afternoon in winter.

Things to See & Do

- Take a walking tour of the Old Town.
- Shop the afternoon away in heritage style.
- Enjoy a production at one of the Shaw's four theatres.
- Visit the lavish Royal George for after-show drinks.

Niagara-on-the-Lake Tourism
26 Queen Street
P.O. Box 1043
Niagara-on-the-Lake
ON L0S 1J0
905-468-1950
niagaraonthelake.com

Shaw Festival Theatre
10 Queen's Parade
Niagara-on-the-Lake
ON L0S 1J0
905-468-2172
1-800-511-7429
shawfest.com

designed for carriages and carts, and lined with mature trees and well-tended brick, clapboard and roughcast-covered buildings. Except for the modern dress of tourists, much of Niagara-on-the-Lake still looks like a prosperous colonial town. It's a delightful place to shop and pass the time while awaiting showtime at the Shaw.

The Shaw Festival has long been considered one of Canada's finest theatrical attractions. Originally inspired by the wit and passion of Bernard Shaw, today's festival honours Shaw and classic theatre while also offering bold contemporary work, approximately a dozen diverse plays per season — quirky comedies, riveting dramas, classic musicals and important new work — produced, directed and performed by some of the country's top theatrical talent.

Shaw Festival productions are presented in four theatres. The Festival Theatre, at 10 Queen's Parade, is the Shaw's flagship theatre, hosting major theatrical works and other cultural events. This beautiful proscenium-arch theatre seats 856 and is lined with British Columbia cedar. Also at this address is the Jackie Maxwell Studio Theatre. The 200-seat venue typically offers two plays per season.

The Court House Theatre, at 26 Queen Street, dates to the 1840s and is a National Historic Site. The Shaw Festival began at the Court House in 1962. The building's upper level combines an intimate 327-seat auditorium with a thrust stage.

The Royal George Theatre, 85 Queen Street, seats 313. It was built as a vaudeville house to entertain troops stationed in Niagara-on-the-Lake during the First World War. The modest-fronted Royal George is all Edwardian gilt mouldings, red walls and golden lions inside. The basement bar and lounge are lined with black-and-white photographs from past productions.

49

NIAGARA FALLS
~ Niagara Falls

When people speak of Niagara Falls, they invariably mean Horseshoe Falls. By far the largest of the three falls in the Niagara Gorge, this waterfall has a span of 790 metres (2,592 ft) and a vertical drop of 57 metres (186 ft). The two smaller — but still impressive — falls are the American Falls and Bridal Veil Falls, both located on the U.S. side of the border.

These falls were created about 10,000 years ago when glaciers receded at the end of the most recent ice age. While not among the world's highest waterfalls, Horseshoe Falls is so wide that an average 2.4 million litres of water per second (634,000 gal) thunders over its crest, placing it in the top five in terms of volume and making it the most powerful waterfall in North America. (About half of this volume is currently diverted for hydroelectric power.)

There are several exciting ways to experience this natural wonder. Journey Behind the Falls starts with an elevator ride down through 45 metres (150 ft) of bedrock to tunnels that lead to the Cataract Portal and Great Falls Portal. Here, you can stand behind the wall of water as it crashes 13 storeys to the basin below.

Hornblower Niagara Cruises offers a Great Gorge Tour aboard a state-of-the-art 700-person catamaran. The trip takes you past American Falls and Bridal Veil Falls and eventually into the roar and mist of magnificent Horseshoe Falls.

The White Water Walk leads visitors along a boardwalk at the foot of the falls. Two observation areas at the edge of the river provide breathtaking views of the

Things to See & Do

- Experience the thunderous Journey Behind the Falls.
- Ride the Falls Incline Railway between Table Rock and the Fallsview Tourist Area.
- Tread the boardwalk, and watch the river accelerate toward the falls.
- Face the falls aboard the Hornblower tour boat.

Niagara Parks
  Commission
Oak Hall
P.O. Box 150
7400 Portage Road
  South
Niagara Falls, ON
L2E 6T2
905-356-2241
1-877-642-7275
niagaraparks.com

TOP LEFT: The Whirlpool Aero Car crosses the Niagara River above the Whirlpool Rapids. BOTTOM LEFT: The pot of gold is clearly aboard the Hornblower Cruises boat skirting the powerful falls. BELOW: A panoramic view of both the American and Canadian (Horseshoe) falls at sunset.

Whirlpool Rapids. These class 6 rapids boast four kilometres (2.5 km) of standing waves approximately three to five metres high (10–16 ft), making this white-water stretch the largest series of standing waves in North America.

Finally, the Whirlpool Aero Car, a cable car that has been in operation since 1916, is a great way to look directly into the eye of the raging Niagara Whirlpool. The car carries 35 standing passengers along sturdy steel cables on a 10-minute round trip.

50

NIAGARA WINE COUNTRY
~ Niagara Peninsula

Ontario's most active wine region owes its distinctive microclimate to the Niagara Escarpment. The almost 100 vineyards nestled between the historic communities of Grimsby and Niagara-on-the-Lake are protected by the Escarpment's high cliffs, which create a cool but temperate climate similar to that of northern California, northern France and Germany.

Grapes grown in cooler regions ripen and accumulate flavour more slowly than those grown in warmer regions. As a result, Niagara wines tend to be complex, with balanced acidity and more mineral overtones. The climate favours certain grape varieties, particularly pinot noir, gamay noir, chardonnay, riesling and cabernet franc.

Given the number of wineries in the area, figuring out where to start can be a challenge. If you have a favourite type of wine (a varietal), you might choose to tour wineries that specialize in that grape. The winecountryontario.ca Wine Route Planner can help you make the most of your excursion. Do a little research, talk to friends who've spent time in the region, then head for a winery that has captured your interest and add a few nearby wineries to fill out your day.

A terrific way to tour Niagara's wine country is by bicycle. The region's cycling routes are a mixture of level and gently rolling terrain, primarily on bike paths and well-maintained country roads. Bike tours are also available through

FACING PAGE: A Niagara peninsula vineyard under a dramatic late-afternoon sky. BELOW, LEFT TO RIGHT: Grapes, ripe and ready for harvest; wine being aged in oak barrels; a professional sommelier pours wine at Konzelmann Estate Winery.

Things to See & Do

- Cycle the Niagara Wine Route.
- Experience a tour and tasting.
- Learn how to match food and wine.
- Attend up to three festivals.

VQA Wines
   of Ontario and
   Wine Country Ontario
4890 Victoria
   Avenue North
P.O. Box 4000
Vineland, ON L0R 2E0
905-562-8070
   Ext. 221
winecountryontario.ca

Niagara Grape
   & Wine Festival
8 Church Street
Suite 100
St. Catharines, ON
L2R 3B3
905-688-0212
niagarawinefestival.com

several local companies. The Niagara Region Bicycle Map is available as an iPhone app and uses GPS technology to show your location on the map.

Niagara's wine industry hosts three different festivals. The Niagara Icewine Festival takes place over three weekends in January and celebrates this award-winning product in winter fashion, with a gala and numerous outdoor activities. The Niagara Homegrown Wine Festival heralds the start of summer in June, as award-winning winemakers open their cellar doors to share their "New Vintage" experience with visitors. Finally, September's Grape & Wine Festival features more than 100 events to toast the harvest, including concerts, street parades, food pairings by top chefs and individual winery celebrations.

51

"ONTARIO'S BEST-PRESERVED MAIN STREET"

～ Port Hope

S ituated on the north shore of Lake Ontario in Northumberland County, Port Hope is a "preserved-heritage" community. TVOntario viewers voted Walton Street the "Best Preserved Main Street in Ontario."

An economic boom in the mid-1800s led to the development of numerous three- and four-storey brick commercial buildings and dozens of Cape Cod-style residences that still stand today. The Ganaraska River runs through town, featuring several kilometres of waterfront trails and a sandy beach. Trinity College

Downtown Port Hope's historic John Street, seen here at dusk.

Fishermen try their luck from the shore of the Ganaraska River as it flows past the Lantern Inn in downtown Port Hope.

School, one of Canada's oldest and most respected private educational institutions, is pristinely maintained. Older houses are restored rather than torn down. Residents take great pride in tending to their plots of land, and Port Hope is home to some award-winning gardens. Many artists call this town home, enjoying its numerous galleries, antique shops, festivals, restaurants and cafés.

The local theatre, the Capitol, is now a National Historic Site. Constructed in 1930 with an interior designed to resemble a medieval courtyard surrounded by a forest, it was one of the first cinemas in the country built for "talking pictures." The Capitol operates as both a movie theatre and as a stage for live theatrical productions. The early-20th-century Art Deco influence is evident in the paint colours and in the stencils used in the lobby and auditorium. From the inner lobby, with its original furniture, one climbs the steps to the auditorium, where the frescoed walls and ceiling suggest the theatre's castle courtyard through the use of faux-plaster walls finished in 17 different colours.

Port Hope is also home to the annual three-day Vintage Film Festival and the All-Canadian Jazz Festival (also three days), a tented event that celebrates and supports the Canadian jazz community with a uniquely Canadian line-up and some of the biggest names in Canadian jazz.

To commemorate the devastating flood that swept through Port Hope's downtown in 1980, each spring the community holds the Float Your Fanny Down the Ganny race on the Ganaraska River, a 10-kilometre (6.2 mi) race that draws crowds of up to 15,000 spectators. Participants range from serious paddlers, who navigate the swift water in kayaks and canoes, to "crazy craft" paddlers, who propel the most inventive watercraft imaginable down the river toward the finish line.

Things to See & Do

- Stroll the best-preserved main street in Ontario.
- Attend the Vintage Film Festival at the Capitol Theatre.
- Catch a concert at the All-Canadian Jazz Festival.
- Attend the wacky Float Your Fanny Down the Ganny race.

Visit Port Hope
20 Queen Street
Port Hope, ON
L1A 2Y7
905-885-2004
1-888-767-8467
visitporthope.ca

52

REMEMBRANCE PARK
～ Georgetown/Halton Hills

Located a block west of Main Street in downtown Georgetown, Remembrance Park is representative of the hundreds of community military memorials and cenotaphs found in Ontario. Each city, town and village in the province finds its own way to honour the bravery of its citizens in times of war and conflict and to remember the fallen. Remembrance Park exudes a deep sense of pride and strength, while inviting contemplation.

The original memorial was erected in 1920, in memory of the local men who died in the First World War. It was updated with additional plaques following the Second World War and the Korean War. In 1960, the memorial was moved to its current location, and in 2000, Remembrance Park was part of a major restoration and beautification program.

Atop the central memorial is a large statue of an angel of peace taming a lion. On each side of the statue's stone base is a plaque commemorating local residents who fell during the three aforementioned wars. A fourth plaque has been added for the casualties of subsequent conflicts. Fountains border the cenotaph.

The citizens of this area are particularly proud of the soldiers who paid the ultimate sacrifice as members of the brave Lorne Scots (Peel, Dufferin and Halton Regiment) "Halton Company," part of a Primary Reserve infantry regiment that served in the South African War, the First and Second World Wars, NATO operations and the War on Terror. They were also involved in peacekeeping operations

Remembrance Park's central memorial, an angel of peace taming a lion, with artillery cannon in the foreground.

ABOVE: Members of the Lorne Scots (Peel, Dufferin and Halton Regiment) pay tribute to the fallen.
RIGHT: Veterans Walk includes trailside plaques listing soldiers' names and details of their deaths.

Things to See & Do

- Attend a Remembrance Day ceremony in Remembrance Park.
- Read the plaques on the cenotaph and along the walkway.
- Walk among the gardens and think of the veterans in your family.
- Visit a military memorial near you and pay your respects.

Remembrance Park
29 James Street
Georgetown, ON
L7G 2H2
905-702-1787
haltonhills.ca/parks/
DestinationParks.php

in the Middle East, Golan Heights, Namibia, Cambodia, Cyprus, the former Yugoslavia and Afghanistan.

In addition to the names listed on the memorial, trailside plaques list soldiers' names and details of their deaths. The stone walkways have shaded benches, and a pair of artillery cannons rest silently amid beautiful floral gardens, maintained by the Dutch Canadian Remembrance Committee.

Here are a few other Ontario military memorials worth visiting: The Battle of Crysler's Hill Memorial, Morrisburg; the Canadian Volunteer Monument, Ontario Veterans Memorial, Old City Hall Cenotaph, Toronto; the Garden of the Unforgotten, Oshawa; Stoney Creek Battlefield Memorial, Hamilton; the Camp X Memorial, Whitby; the Great War Memorial, Niagara Falls; the Korean War Memorial, Brampton; the Welland-Crowland War Memorial, Welland; and, in Ottawa, the Commonwealth Air Force Monument, the National Aboriginal Veterans Monument, the Canadian National War Memorial ("The Response"), the Royal Canadian Navy Monument, the Valiants Memorial, the Peacekeeping Monument, and the East and West Memorial Buildings (housing the Department of Veterans Affairs).

53 ROYAL BOTANICAL GARDENS
~ Burlington

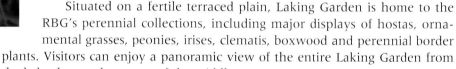

Protected by the Niagara Escarpment, Burlington's Royal Botanical Gardens (RBG) contains four distinct gardens and 27 kilometres (17 mi) of trails within a nature reserve that extends over some 1,100 hectares (2,718 acres). They are the largest botanical gardens in Canada.

The main entrance leads visitors through Stedman Exploration Hall into the RBG Centre, where highlights include a living wall in the Camilla and Peter Dalglish Atrium, the large Mediterranean Garden and an extensive cacti and succulent collection.

Things to See & Do

- Visit the living wall in the Camilla and Peter Dalglish Atrium.
- Travel from the Centennial Rose Garden to the Prehistoric Grove.
- Take home countless new ideas from the Rock Garden.
- Visit the Arboretum when the trees peak in spring and fall.

Royal Botanical Gardens
680 Plains Road West
Burlington, ON
L7T 4H4
905-527-1158
1-800-694-4769
rbg.ca

The next stop, Hendrie Park, can be accessed through an underground tunnel. Hendrie Park garden emphasizes diversity among plants and garden designs. The more formal Centennial Rose Garden runs either side of the garden's reflecting pools, and the White Garden and the Lily Collection add further elegance. But Hendrie also houses the Prehistoric Grove, the Medieval Garden and the Medicinal Garden, as well as native plants in a cultivated setting, a fascinating Global Garden and new ideas for vegetable gardening in Veggie Village.

Situated on a fertile terraced plain, Laking Garden is home to the RBG's perennial collections, including major displays of hostas, ornamental grasses, peonies, irises, clematis, boxwood and perennial border plants. Visitors can enjoy a panoramic view of the entire Laking Garden from the belvedere at the centre of the middle terrace.

The rejuvenated David Braley and Nancy Gordon Rock Garden features new paths with gentler grades designed to be accessible to all guests. Upgraded lighting and sound allow for extended hours and more special events. Attuned to the challenges of climate change, the RGB gardeners keep in mind plant selection, design and management that promotes pollinator-friendly plants, native Ontario species and drought-tolerant perennials, while maintaining the lively seasonal colours and textures of a world-class rock garden.

The fourth garden, RBG's Arboretum, resembles an English landscape park, where visitors can see a wide variety of trees and other woody plants up close. Two Arboretum landmarks are Rasberry House — named for the family who operated a market garden and dairy farm on this site for nearly 100 years — and its adjacent silo. The charming old house on the hill to the north serves as the headquarters for the Bruce Trail Association.

The RBG offers over 200 courses and workshops for families, kids and adults in the areas of gardening, nature, botanical arts and wellness. It also hopes to provide gardeners with inspiration and ideas that will help them make their home gardens more interesting, efficient and sustainable. ~

LEFT: The pineapple-topped fountain in Hendrie Park Gardens. BELOW: Trailside tulips in bloom at the RBG, which has been designated a National Historic Site. FACING PAGE: Summer peonies at the Royal Botanical Gardens.

54

SOUND OF MUSIC FESTIVAL
∿ Burlington

Things to See & Do

- Take in one of the 100 performances on 10 stages over nine days.
- Hear Canadian rock icons.
- Discover top local indie artists.
- Enjoy the pedestrian-only Streetfest.

Sound of Music Festival
Box 85007
561 Brant Street
Burlington, ON
L7R 4K3
905-333-6364
soundofmusic.ca

E ach June, Burlington plays host to "Canada's Largest Free Music Festival." Disclaimer: Not every performance is free — the epic big-name multi-artist kick-off concert is ticketed — but most of the 100 acts that perform on 10 stages over the festival's nine days can be seen and heard without an admission fee.

Burlington's popular Sound of Music Festival encompasses Father's Day weekend, with events distributed through Spencer Smith Park along the city's waterfront and extending into the downtown core. The festival received Ontario Tourism's "Event of the Year" award for 2016 — one of many awards it has garnered in recent years.

Saturday's kick-off concert brings big talent to the park's main stage. From Sunday to Wednesday, the Club Series' spotlight is on local talent, with nightly performances in downtown bars and restaurants. And on Thursday, the free concerts start in earnest, with entertainment on every stage and every corner.

The festival supports music of diverse genres, with dozens of local and regional artists delivering rock, blues, R&B, urban, folk, roots and country in street, stage and club performances. But the focus is on Canadian music. Headline artists have included The Offspring, Marianas Trench, Tom Cochrane, The Spin Doctors, USS, The Road Hammers, Faber Drive, Finger Eleven, Sloan, Men Without Hats, The Tea Party, Carly Rae Jepsen, The Trews, Jacksoul, Terra Lightfoot, The Mahones, Moist, Bedouin Soundclash, Great Lake Swimmers, Walk Off the Earth, Wintersleep and These Kids Wear Crowns.

The festival's 800 volunteers welcome more than 200,000 guests, and while the emphasis is on music, visitors will also enjoy the Downtown Streetfest, the Grande Festival Parade, the midway carnival, a Kids' Zone and the wide range of vendors. ∿

RIGHT: Moist performs at Burlington's annual Sound of Music Festival. FACING PAGE: Events along the city's waterfront and extending into the downtown core attract thousands to "Canada's Largest Free Music Festival."

EASTERN ONTARIO

55 ~ Bon Echo Provincial Park & Mazinaw Rock | Near Kaladar

56 ~ Bonnechere Caves & Fourth Chute Falls | Eganville

57 ~ Family Day on the Waterway | Brockville

58 ~ Fort Henry National Historic Site | Kingston

59 ~ Fort Wellington National Historic Site &
Battle of the Windmill National Historic Site | Prescott

60 ~ Historic Perth | Perth

61 ~ Kingston City Hall | Kingston

62 ~ Marmora SnoFest & Sled-Dog Races | Marmora

63 ~ North Frontenac Dark Sky Preserve | South of Plevna

64 ~ Pembroke's Heritage Murals | Pembroke

65 ~ Sandbanks Provincial Park | Prince Edward County

66 ~ The County | Prince Edward County

67 ~ Thousand Islands National Park | St. Lawrence River

68 ~ Upper Canada Village | Morrisburg

OTTAWA

69 ~ ByWard Market | Ottawa

70 ~ Canada Day on Parliament Hill | Ottawa

71 ~ Canadian Museum of Nature | Ottawa

72 ~ Canadian Tulip Festival | Ottawa

73 ~ Rideau Canal National Historic Site | Ottawa–Kingston

74 ~ Winterlude | Ottawa

Quebec

ByWard
Market

Downtown

Sandy Hill

Centretown

Old
Ottawa
East

The Glebe

Algonquin
Provincial
Park

Pembroke 64

Eganville 56

Quebec

Ottawa

Plevna

55

63

Perth 60

Morrisburg 68

Prescott 59

Kaladar

Brockville 57

62 Marmora

67

Napanee

61 58

Belleville

Kingston

Trenton

66

Picton

65

Lake Ontario

U.S.A.

N

W   E

S

55

BON ECHO PROVINCIAL PARK & MAZINAW ROCK

~ Near Kaladar

ABOVE: A few of the more than 250 red ochre paintings left by ancient Algonquin ancestors on Mazinaw Rock and nearby outcrops. The paintings are thought to be among the oldest on the Canadian Shield. FACING PAGE: Canoeing below the high cliffs of Mazinaw Rock at sunset. FOLLOWING PAGES: The rocky shorelines and clinging conifers of Bon Echo Provincial Park give it a decidedly northern feel.

Although easily reached from most southern and eastern Ontario communities, Bon Echo Provincial Park can often make you feel like you're farther north. The rocky shorelines of its lakes, the dense pines and the stunningly clear night skies make Bon Echo a great destination for those who want to escape civilization on short notice.

Camping options in Bon Echo come in all forms: canoe-in sites, trail-access sites, walk-in sites, car-camping and RV sites, cabins, soft-sided shelters and yurts. Three natural sand beaches offer swimming, and Joeperry and Pearson lakes are motorboat-free and feature 25 canoe-in campsites for paddlers. Joeperry Lake has its own sandy beach.

The park's several hiking trails range from an easy one-kilometre (.6 mi) stroll along Bon Echo Creek to the moderate-to-difficult Abes and Essens Lake Trail, which comprises three interconnecting looped trails totalling about 30 kilometres (18.6 mi). There are five reservable campsites along the latter. Views are particularly spectacular in fall.

Cliff Top Trail on Mazinaw Lake is accessible only by water. You can canoe or kayak to the trailhead (both types of watercraft are available to rent) or pay a modest fee to be taken there by ferry. This hike to the top of famous Mazinaw Rock features three lake-view observation decks.

Excluding the Great Lakes, Mazinaw Lake is the second-deepest lake in

Things to See & Do

- Visit the Mazinaw Rock pictographs.
- Hike the Cliff Top Trail.
- Canoe the countless coves of Joeperry Lake.
- Watch for endangered peregrine falcons.

Bon Echo Provincial Park
16151 Highway 41
Cloyne, ON K0H 1K0
613-336-2228
ontarioparks.com/park/ bonecho

Ontario, and Mazinaw Rock's stately cliffs rise 100 metres (330 ft) from its surface. Here, hundreds of years ago, ancestors of the Algonquin people etched more than 250 images on 65 rock surfaces using red ochre. These ancient pictographs represent human and animal figures, as well as abstract and geometric designs. It is difficult to accurately date the faded pigment, but the Mazinaw paintings are thought to be the oldest on the Canadian Shield.

Paddlers can head directly to Mazinaw Rock or paddle the 21 kilometres (13 mi) along the Kishkebus canoe loop (rated moderate to difficult), which takes you past the pictographs en route to the nature reserve on the park's east side. Interpretive boat tours are also available.

Peregrine falcons can often seen nesting on Mazinaw Rock. Birders should also watch for great crested flycatchers, kestrels and red-tailed hawks.

56

BONNECHERE CAVES & FOURTH CHUTE FALLS

~ Eganville

Since opening to the public in 1955, the Bonnechere Caves have attracted thousands of visitors from all over the world. Located in the hamlet of Fourth Chute, beside the Bonnechere River near the village of Eganville, the Bonnechere Caves are among the best examples of solution caves in North America. Solution caves occur when acidic groundwater scours surrounding rock — in this case, limestone — over a long period of time.

The process began approximately 10,000 years ago, toward the end of the most recent ice age. As the glaciers retreated, the waters we now call the Bonnechere River began etching their way ever deeper into the surface rock.

BELOW: Bonnechere Caves are among the best examples of solution caves in North America. FACING PAGE: A lighted boardwalk leads through layers of limestone first deposited in the ancient sea as silt, mud and organic sediment roughly 485 to 445 million years ago.

Things to See & Do

- Explore one of the best solution caves in North America.
- Locate 450-million-year-old marine fossils.
- Visit scenic Fourth Chute Falls.

Bonnechere Caves
1237 Fourth Chute Road
Eganville, ON K0J 1T0
613-628-2283
1-800-469-2283
bonnecherecaves.com

As you explore the caves along the lighted boardwalk, you will see countless layers of exposed limestone. These layers were first deposited in the ancient sea as silt, mud and organic sediment during the Ordovician Period, roughly 485 to 445 million years ago. The time-scale is mind-boggling. What you are looking at existed 200 million years before the first dinosaurs. It was a period during which diverse marine invertebrates, including trilobites and brachiopods and early vertebrates, such as conodonts, thrived alongside primitive fish, cephalopods, corals, crinoids and gastropods. The fossilized remains of many of these early creatures can be seen at Bonnechere.

Bonnechere Caves is a family-owned and -operated site, and there is a modest charge for the informative and geologically humbling hour-long guided tour.

The Fourth Chute, one of five waterfalls on the Bonnechere River, is located adjacent to Bonnechere Caves' picnic area. Trails allow numerous vantage points, and flat rocks encourage leisurely viewing. The Fourth Chute is a "stepped plunge" waterfall with two steps for a combined height of about 10 metres (33 ft). The lower falls is the more dramatic of the two, with the river coursing over several prominent rock ledges.

Fourth Chute Falls drops twice, for a combined height of 10 metres (33 ft). The surrounding flat rocks afford plenty of excellent viewing locations.

57 FAMILY DAY ON THE WATERWAY
∼ Brockville

Brockville offers families many ways to enjoy a day along the historic St. Lawrence River, beginning with a trip to the Aquatarium at Tall Ships Landing. This 2,508-square-metre (27,000 sq ft) climate-controlled aquarium and discovery centre showcases the diversity of St. Lawrence habitat. Visitors can view a variety of fish species up close as they walk through the Aquatarium's underwater tunnel. Plan to be around for the otters' morning or afternoon feeding. Suspended 3.7 metres (12 ft) above the third floor, the Aquatarium's Ropes Experience lets you traverse an obstacle adventure course through the rigging of a tall ship. It's a great way to build confidence while learning about the historic ships of the St. Lawrence. Walk the wooden plank and take the 12-metre (40 ft) AquaDrop "leap of faith" from the fourth floor to the first floor, or opt for a comfortable slide off the SS *Kingston*.

The south entrance to Canada's First Railway Tunnel is located at Armagh Sifton Price Park, directly south of City Hall at Water Street. Completed in 1860 for the Brockville & Ottawa Railway, the tunnel is arch-shaped, measuring 4.5 metres (14 ft 9 in) high and 4.3 metres (14 ft) across, with an overall length of 525 metres (1,721 ft). It passes directly beneath Brockville City Hall and Brockville's downtown core. A new paved floor and state-of-the-art energy-efficient

TOP: The obstacle adventure course is suspended from the rigging of a tall ship at the Aquatarium. ABOVE: The interactive Water Table play area. RIGHT: Visitors watch as a diver swims above them in the Aquatarium's underwater tunnel.

Boldt Castle, shown above, and Singer Castle are a featured part of most Brockville-based tours and cruises.

Things to See & Do

- Try Aquatarium's Ropes Experience in the rigging of a tall ship.
- Walk under City Hall in Canada's First Railway Tunnel.
- Take a cruise on the St. Lawrence River.
- Visit the mansion and gardens of Brockville's Fulford family.

Brockville Tourism
10 Market Street West
Brockville, ON K6V 4R7
613-342-4357
1-888-251-7676
brockvilletourism.com
thegreatwaterway.com/
pt-destination/
brockville

lighting highlight the tunnel's architecture. The bottom and top thirds of the tunnel are completely lined with stone. The unlined centre third is exposed rock, where dripping water has created colourful mineral deposits along the walls. Unique wooden doors at either end allow the tunnel to be opened and closed. Brockville's new Railway Tunnel Park will become the central hub of the city's Brock Trail recreational pathway.

This is river-cruise country, and Brockville-based 1000 Islands & Seaway Cruises operates a fleet of modern, Transport Canada-certified vessels. Its high-speed catamaran presents an adventurous alternative to the traditional sightseeing cruise, whisking passengers into the heart of the Thousand Islands for a two-hour "AdrenIsland" cruise that includes views of both Boldt and Singer castles. In off-peak seasons, 1000 Islands & Seaway Cruises offer traditional Canal and Seaway tours, including full-day and two-day cruises.

Fulford Place National Historic Site is a 1,858-square-metre (20,000 sq ft) Edwardian mansion built for Senator George Taylor Fulford, who made his millions from "Pink Pills for Pale People," a patent medicine manufactured in Brockville, advertised in mass-circulation newspapers and sold worldwide. Constructed between 1899 and 1901, the grand Beaux Arts-style house still contains many of the tapestries, paintings, statuary and ceramics collected on the Fulfords' world travels. The original grounds were designed by Frederick Olmsted, whose firm also designed Central Park in New York City. Ontario Heritage Trust undertook restoration of the Italianate-style heritage gardens with their elaborate triton fountain, statuary, stonewalls and gates.

58

FORT HENRY NATIONAL HISTORIC SITE
～ Kingston

Located on Kingston's Point Henry, where the Cataraqui River flows into the St. Lawrence River at the east end of Lake Ontario, Fort Henry is a National Historic Site of Canada and in 2007 was included in the Rideau Canal's designation as a UNESCO World Heritage Site.

The original Fort Henry was built on this strategic point during the War of 1812 and then replaced by a larger structure in the 1830s, following the completion of the Rideau Canal. The expanded fort was to be part of a defensive system designed to protect Canada's essential trade routes.

British troops were deployed to Fort Henry from 1813 to 1870, at which time British Army garrisons were replaced by Canadian troops. But with no active threats from foreign foes, the fort eventually fell into disrepair. However, between 1936 and 1938, under a government work program tied to the Great Depression, Ronald L. Way directed the restoration of Fort Henry as a living history museum. Today, the largest fortification west of Quebec City operates as an authentic replica of a Confederation-

LEFT: Fort Henry's marching band on parade in full dress. BELOW: Fort Henry, up on the hill, with one of its Martello towers in the foreground. FACING PAGE: A cannoneer's view. The fort guards a strategic point where the Cataraqui River flows into the St. Lawrence.

era British military fortress — with a bit of assistance from modern technology.

Through guest-triggered exhibits, the fort's high-tech Discovery Centre offers visitors the opportunity to interact with some of the 19th-century figures who helped shape Canada's history. You can also watch authentically costumed re-enactors perform the daily chores of the era, set your watch by the Noon Gun, and witness the Fort Henry Guard perform military music, drills and artillery practices. (You can even fire a rifle yourself.) And the Victorian School Room holds classes every day at 11:30 a.m., 1:00 p.m. and 3:45 p.m. during summer. Practise writing a letter home from 1867 Kingston or listen to storytelling sessions.

If you proceed along the east wall, you may encounter the Fort Henry Guard's goat mascot, David X. To commemorate the mascot of the 23rd Regiment of Foot (Royal Welch Fusiliers), stationed at Fort Henry in 1842 and 1843, the Saint David Society of Toronto has donated the previous nine white Saanen goats to Fort Henry since 1953. Using Roman numerals, the current goat is David X. He can be seen on walks around the fort, as well as in parades and other Guard celebrations.

Every Wednesday evening in July and August, the day ends with the World Heritage Sunset Ceremonies, in which the Fort Henry Guard Drum Corps, Drill Squad and Artillery Detachments present a grand display of 1860s military rituals. The performance can be heard throughout downtown Kingston.

Things to See & Do

- Learn about the strategic importance of Fort Henry.
- Watch the Guard do drills and use period artillery.
- Meet the Guard's goat mascot.
- Attend a Heritage Sunset Ceremony.

Fort Henry National Historic Site
1 Fort Henry Drive
Kingston, ON K7K 5G8
613-542-7388
1-800-437-2233
forthenry.com

59

FORT WELLINGTON NATIONAL HISTORIC SITE & BATTLE OF THE WINDMILL NATIONAL HISTORIC SITE

∼ Prescott

Located on the north shore of the St. Lawrence River at Prescott, Fort Wellington was commissioned by the British government to protect the head of the Gallop Rapids during the War of 1812. Prior to the creation of the St. Lawrence Seaway in the 1950s, a series of rapids ran downriver from Prescott to Montreal. Since it was impossible to negotiate the rapids in full-sized lake ships, freight and passengers bound for Montreal or Kingston had to be distributed among smaller bateaux for this stretch of the journey. And since Prescott is directly across the river from Ogdensburg, New York, it was vulnerable to potential military action by the United States. Prescott was also a communications hub for the rest of Upper Canada.

Fort Wellington was constructed in 1813 on land owned by Major Edward Jessup, the prominent Connecticut Loyalist who had founded Prescott in 1784. The fort would help thwart another American invasion, during the Rebellions of 1837–38, as part of the Battle of the Windmill.

BELOW, LEFT TO RIGHT: A view from the gates inside Fort Wellington; a British battlefield band plays during a re-enactment of the War of 1812; through the tunnel and into the fort; American Patriot re-enactors fire their flintlock rifles.

In November of 1838, a force of Patriot "Hunters" met at Sackets Harbor, New York, and made their way downriver to Ogdensburg aboard civilian vessels. Their plan was to seize Fort Wellington and then organize the disaffected citizens of Upper Canada into a Patriot-led army that would depose the British governor of the colony. The Hunters' actions had to be undertaken in secrecy, as the American government would not condone an attack by Americans on the Canadas when no state of war existed.

But British spies had managed to infiltrate the Hunters and report their location and the approximate timing for the attack on Prescott. A militia of 250 well-armed Hunters encountered some 600 advancing British troops. Further dimming the Hunters' chances was the fact that the support they had anticipated from discontented Canadians failed to materialize. The Canadian colonies weren't interested in being liberated.

The battle marked a brief, bloody turning point in Canadian history, and the tower and grounds are now preserved as the Battle of the Windmill Historic Site. The stone windmill still stands, 19 metres (60 ft) tall atop a nine-metre (30 ft) slope. It was converted to a lighthouse in 1873.

Fort Wellington retained a regular garrison of British soldiers after the Rebellion. Today, visitors can see the fort restored to its circa 1846 condition, when the garrison comprised a Royal Artillery detachment and a company from the Royal Canadian Rifle Regiment. Uniformed guides conduct tours of the fortifications and buildings, including the storerooms and barracks in the blockhouse. The fort's military museum is found on the third floor of the blockhouse. A Visitor Centre showcases an 1812-era gunboat wreck as well as exhibits about the fort's history.

Visitors are welcome to explore the gunboat, try on period military costumes, take part in military drills, witness the firing of the cannons, sample period treats cooked over an open fire and play 19th-century games.

Things to See & Do

- Don a period military uniform and take part in a drill.
- Learn the details of the historic Battle of the Windmill.
- Climb the Windmill Tower for a spectacular view of the St. Lawrence.
- Witness the firing of the cannons.

Fort Wellington National HIstoric Site
370 Vankoughnet Street
Prescott, ON K0E 1T0
613-925-2896
1-888-773-8888
pc.gc.ca/en/lhn-nhs/on/wellington

60

HISTORIC PERTH
∼ Perth

Located on the Tay River, 83 kilometres (52 mi) southwest of Ottawa, Perth is the seat of Lanark County. The town was established as a military settlement in 1816, and many of its first residents were British military veterans from the War of 1812. The first Scottish settlers arrived that year as well, many of them stonemasons who came to work on the locks of the Rideau Canal and on prominent buildings in the area. A good number of downtown Perth's businesses operate in well-preserved historic stone buildings that date to the 1800s.

Perth's heritage downtown core consists of boutiques, craft stores, antique stores, specialty shops and restaurants. There is a flea market and a Farmers' and Craft Market, the latter housed on summer Saturdays in the distinctive Crystal

Examples of heritage buildings line the Tay Canal. The town of Perth got its start as a military settlement in 1816.

Palace. The country-modern Crystal Palace stands out among all the historic stone. It was built from discarded remnants of glass street enclosures once found on Rideau Street in Ottawa.

The grand Matheson House, at 11 Gore Street East, is now the Perth Museum, with four rooms restored to their 1840s appearance. The museum also houses the pistols used in the "Last Fatal Duel in Upper Canada," which was fought between two young law students on the banks of the Tay River on June 13, 1833, for a lady's honour.

Perth is home to Canada's oldest pioneer burial ground, the St. Paul's United Church Cemetery (formerly the Old Methodist Burying Ground). This cemetery is at the southeast end of Last Duel Park on Robinson Street. Craig Street Cemetery, sometimes referred to as the "Old Burying Grounds," was used between 1820 and 1873 and also contains many historic graves.

The first installation of a telephone, other than Alexander Graham Bell's experimental installations, occurred in Perth. Town dentist Dr. J. F. Kennedy, a friend of Bell, had a direct telephone connection installed between his home and office. By 1887, there were 19 telephones in Perth, with the switchboard located in Dr. Kennedy's office.

Perth's Scottish heritage is celebrated at the former Links O'Tay Golf & Country Club, now the Perth Golf Course. Founded in 1890, it claims to be the oldest continuously operating golf course on the same site in Canada. It is also celebrated through the annual "Kilt Run." In 2010, 1,089 kilt-clad runners crossed the finish line to set a Guinness World Record. The eight-kilometre (5 mi) Kilt Run was organized to commemorate the 800th anniversary of Perth, Scotland, but the "Perth World Record Kilt Run," as it is now known, has since become an ever-expanding annual event, with Ontario's Perth and Scotland's Perth vying for the most kilted participants. The 2015 Kilt Run attracted 2,800 registered runners.

Things to See & Do

- Admire the work of Scottish stonemasons in downtown Perth.
- Visit the Farmers' and Craft Market in the Crystal Palace.
- Dine along the Tay River.
- Don a kilt for the Perth World Record Kilt Run.

Town Hall
80 Gore Street East
Perth, ON K7H 1H9
613-267-3311
perth.ca

BELOW LEFT: Stately Perth Town Hall was built in 1863–64 and is designated a National Historic Site of Canada.
BELOW RIGHT: Picturesque Stewart Park, with its Rainbow Bridge, has helped make Perth the "Wedding Capital of Eastern Ontario."

61

KINGSTON CITY HALL
~ Kingston

Construction of Kingston City Hall and Market began in 1842. The previous year, Kingston had been selected as the capital of the new United Province of Canada, and it was thought that this structure should reflect the city's stature as the seat of government.

Belfast-born George Browne designed the building and would go on to become one of Canada's leading 19th-century architects. It was an ambitious project. The town hall, municipal offices, post office, customs house, police station, market hall and mechanics' institute were all to be housed under one roof. The project's epic scale reflected the city's pride in its new status and potential growth.

The T-shaped building, a superb example of Neoclassical civic architecture, has three wings that are joined at a central core, which supports a dome and belfry. The dome and massive portico dominate the building's main façade.

Of course, by the time construction was completed in 1844, Montreal had taken over as the capital city. Kingston City Hall was nevertheless an impressive sight, occupying a full city block facing Lake Ontario in the downtown district, and it is considered one of Browne's most outstanding works. After his death in 1891, Sir John A. Macdonald, Canada's first prime minister and former Kingston alderman, lay in state in what is now Memorial Hall until his interment in Kingston's Cataraqui Cemetery.

City Hall housed the city's original police headquarters, with workspaces for the constables and several dark, cramped basement cells to hold the men, women and children arrested on suspicion of crimes. These cells remained in use until 1906 and still speak volumes about 19th-century policing techniques. Efforts have been made to restore the office area and cells as historical examples of Canada's early criminal-justice system.

In 1921, 12 stained-glass windows in Memorial Hall were dedicated in honour of Kingston's sailors, soldiers, airmen and nursing sisters who served overseas in the First World War. In 1961, Kingston City Hall was designated a National Historic Site.

Confederation Park separates City Hall from the waterfront. Established in 1967 on former industrial land, the lakeside park is a natural site for events, boasting an attractive arch and fountain. It also overlooks the downtown marina. The former Kingston & Pembroke Railway station now serves as a visitor information centre, and the restored locomotive the *Spirit of Sir John A.* is a reminder of Kingston's locomotive-manufacturing past. ~

BELOW: When construction began on Kingston City Hall, the city was meant to be the capital of the new United Province of Canada. FACING PAGE, TOP: The T-shaped building has three wings that are joined at a central core. The dome and massive portico dominate the building's main façade. FACING PAGE, BOTTOM: The outdoor public market that flourishes today was part of the original 1942 design.

Things to See & Do

- Take a guided tour of this National Historic Site.
- Admire the stained-glass tributes in Memorial Hall.
- Visit the 19th-century jail cells.
- Check out the *Spirit of Sir John A.* in Confederation Park.

Kingston City Hall
216 Ontario Street
Kingston, ON K7L 2Z3
613-546-4291
cityofkingston.ca

62

MARMORA SNOFEST & SLED-DOG RACES

~ Marmora

ABOVE: A carver carefully wields a chainsaw as he competes in the carnival's carving competition. FACING PAGE: SnoFest's perennial favourites, these blue-eyed husky sled dogs are eager to get to work.

Things to See & Do

• Witness the Little Nippers sled-dog races.
• Join local supporters for Marmora's Got Talent.
• Watch the chainsaw carvers in action.
• Contact an outfitter and try mushing your own team.

Marmora SnoFest
P.O. Box 778
Marmora, ON
K0K 2M0
marmorasnofest.ca

D evised to help pull Marmora out of a collective funk, the Marmora SnoFest celebrates a love of dogs, sport and community. It was 1978, and after 27 years of operation, the mighty Marmoraton Mine had closed, laying off hundreds of miners and disrupting numerous service and support businesses. The community needed something positive to get them through the winter. Four decades later, Marmora is still on its feet and proudly hosting its SnoFest winter carnival.

Until recently, Marmora SnoFest was one of the province's top destinations for sled-dog racing and skijoring (a form of racing in which the musher is strapped into cross-country skis and attached to one or two dogs), attracting world-class competitors from across Canada and beyond. In fact, it was home to "Canada's longest-running series of sled-dog races." Alas, climate change and the resultant unpredictable weather have put most of the races on indefinite hiatus. But the tradition will continue in the form of the Little Nippers One-Dog Children-12-and-Under race. Main Street will be closed off and snow and ice will be trucked in from plow piles and the local rink if necessary.

SnoFest opens with the extremely popular and well-attended Marmora's Got Talent variety show, featuring competition in under-13 and 14-and-up divisions. There's also a "Sno-pitch" baseball tournament, an artistic chainsaw carving contest, weight pulls, public skating, the long-running Back of Cordova Curling Challenge, the Artistic Expressions artisan craft show, a Who's Growing Locally farmers' market, a Hastings County-wide chili competition, a silent auction, vendors, a beer tent, bonfires and a SnoFest banquet dinner and dance with live band.

SnoFest's Kidz Zone offers interactive activities, including a live drumming circle, costumed characters, organized games, pony rides, professional storytelling and an inflatable castle and igloo village.

As in most communities, volunteers carry the organizational and operational load. Entry to SnoFest is free, but guests who purchase the $5 SnoFest buttons are greatly appreciated and are entered in a draw for cash prizes.

"We miss the races," said Jennifer Bennett, Tourism and Economic Development Coordinator, nostalgic for predictable winters. "People love the dogs." And the Ontario Federation of Sleddog Sports (OFSS), who supports and helps organize the races, misses losing one of its major annual events. But the OFSS race series hopes to continue to bring some of the fastest sled-dog teams in the world to compete in Ontario events, including the Eldorado Gold Sled Dog Races, the Kearney Dog Sled Races and the Haliburton Highlands Dogsled Derby. ~

63

NORTH FRONTENAC DARK SKY PRESERVE

∼ South of Plevna

RIGHT: The North Frontenac Region experiences some of the most southerly "dark skies" in Canada. With no light pollution, the M33 Triangulum Galaxy (seen here) is visible to the naked eye. For this reason, it is an important marker on the Bortle Dark-Sky Scale. FACING PAGE: The spiral galaxy that we call the Milky Way contains our solar system, as well as an additional 100 to 400 billion other stars and planets.

Ontario has several excellent dark-sky observation sites. And despite population density — and urban light pollution — in the southern part of the province, some of these sites are remarkably accessible. You don't have to go far to see stars.

The North Frontenac region is fortunate to have some of the most southerly "dark skies" in Canada. The Royal Astronomical Society of Canada has designated the darkest region, encompassing the counties of Frontenac, Lennox–Addington, Hastings and Renfrew, as an official Dark Sky Preserve, a naturally isolated area whose residents work to restrict artificial light pollution and to promote astronomy. This is one of the best locations in southern Canada and the northeastern United States for viewing the constellations, with or without a telescope.

The North Frontenac Dark Sky Preserve is also known by its nickname, the "Dark Peninsula." It is a routine destination for both professional and amateur astronomers, who make use of its natural darkness for telescopic surveying. The preserve's website calendar lists dates for major constellation events, including meteor showers and planet sightings.

Things to See & Do

- Go to the dark side. Take your telescope or binoculars.
- Check the website for major dark-sky events.
- See Venus, Mars, Saturn, Jupiter, the Milky Way and more.

North Frontenac
  Municipal Office
6648 Road 506
Plevna, ON K0H 2M0
613-479-2231
1-800-234-3953
northfrontenac.com/
  dark-sky-preserve.html

While you will get a spectacular view of the night sky throughout most of the designated area, there is an official Dark Sky Preserve observation pad located at 5816 Road 506, four kilometres (2.5 mi) southwest of the village of Plevna. The Dark Sky Preserve is very much a public space with parking, amenities, washrooms and electrical service, and anyone can set up a telescope on the concrete observation pad and enjoy the dark skies.

Ontario's other Royal Astronomical Society of Canada-designated preserves include Gordon's Park Dark Sky Preserve, on Manitoulin Island. Gordon's Park is one of the darkest observation sites in the province, with no visible light pollution. Fathom Five Dark Sky Preserve, in the National Marine Park at the northern tip of the Bruce Peninsula, boasts some of the darkest skies in southern Ontario. Point Pelee Dark Sky Preserve, in southwestern Ontario's Essex County, works to curb artificial night lighting, considering it to be an environmental issue that negatively affects local and migrating bird populations as well as nocturnal species. And the Muskoka region's Torrance Barrens Dark Sky Preserve offers dark-sky viewing amid rugged central Ontario cottage country.

64

PEMBROKE'S HERITAGE MURALS
∼ Pembroke

The Upper Ottawa Valley city of Pembroke takes great pride in its history. Samuel de Champlain visited the site in 1613. Through the 1800s, it grew into a vital logging centre. In 1884, it became the first community in Canada to have electric street lighting and an electrically lighted town hall. Today, tourists and visitors can choose from several walking tours that highlight the city's carefully restored historic houses and buildings, its art galleries and its two museums — the Champlain Trail Museum and the Murray L. Moore Hydro Museum. But Pembroke's biggest draw is its many colourful murals.

By design, the murals are an illustrated record of the city's growth and evo-

The Canadian Pacific Railway water tower features a mural (titled *CP Water Tower*, 2000) by John Ellenberger portraying the Prescott waterfront and train depot circa 1950s.

ABOVE LEFT: *The Mayors of Pembroke: A Portrait Gallery, 1877–2014*, by Marilyn Saffery, assisted by Shauna Torgerson; Portraits by Speed Pro Signs, 2012. ABOVE RIGHT: A tribute to *Pembroke Hydro* by Randy Chester, 1990.

Things to See & Do

- Discover the history of Pembroke through its murals.
- Take the self-guided historic walking tour.
- Visit Pembroke's museums.
- Plan an Ontario mural tour with muralroutes.ca

City of Pembroke
1 Pembroke Street East
Pembroke, ON
K8A 3J5
613-735-6821
pembroke.ca/tourism/
 art-and-culture/
 pembroke-heritage-
 murals
muralroutes.ca

lution, as well as a public celebration of the area's rich heritage and traditions. Collectively called "The Pembroke Heritage Murals," they lay claim to being Canada's largest outdoor art gallery. Sides of commercial buildings, some two storeys high, pay tribute to the lumber industry, early settlers, old-time fiddling and step dancing, the blacksmith shop, the Grand Trunk railway station, the full-service gas station, military memories, the city's hockey legacy, and much more.

The first five murals were painted in 1990, and since that time, the Pembroke Heritage Murals committee has overseen the creation of another 30 or so works by artists of local, regional and national stature. Suitably, the artists' styles are as varied as the times and incidents they depict. If you visit during the summer, you are likely to see new murals in progress and older ones being touched up. You may even get an opportunity to talk to the artists about their work. A recent mural, unveiled in 2015 and entitled *Pembroke Farmers Market, 1890–1940*, consists of three free-standing panels located at the current and historic site of the Pembroke Farmers Market, at Lake and Victoria streets. Detailed tour maps are available.

Several other Ontario towns and villages boast noteworthy murals. Midland has at least 35 outdoor murals, including one that is considered to be the largest in North America. Gravenhurst's 14 murals depict the community's history as a logging town and a rail and steamship centre. The town of St. Thomas features 11 railway-themed murals. Other mural communities include Welland, Huntsville, Morrisburg, Athens and Vankleek Hill. And, of course, there are plenty of murals to be found in the Greater Toronto Area. Plan your own tour by using the interactive map at muralroutes.ca.

65

SANDBANKS PROVINCIAL PARK
∼ Prince Edward County

Sandbanks Provincial Park has the largest freshwater barrier dune formation in the world — 1,600 hectares (3,954 acres) of interconnected, ever-shifting sand dunes and unique lagoon habitat — but most visitors come for the beach experience. The park's three main beaches are among the best in Canada for sunning and swimming.

Outlet Beach, in the East Lake section of the park, curves around a large bay and is a favoured spot with families. It's sheltered, the water deepens quite gradually, and the sand is perfect for building sandcastles. The mouth of the Outlet River is one of the park's two designated pet areas, where your four-legged friend can join in the fun and cool off in the lake.

Sandbanks Beach is a narrower, slightly more pebbled beach in the Sandbanks Day-Use area off Lake Ontario. The swimming is comparable

ABOVE: The territorial red-headed woodpecker is considered at risk in Ontario due to habitat loss, but it has been spotted in the open woodland and woodland edges at Sandbanks. RIGHT: Windswept barrier dunes at Sandbanks Provincial Park. FACING PAGE: Another beautiful sunset looking west across Lake Ontario from Sandbanks.

to Outlet Beach, but it is more open to the lake. When the weather turns breezy, it's a great spot for kite flying, kite boarding and windsurfing. Surfers are required to stay 400 metres (437 yd) from designated swimming areas.

Dunes Beach, which is located in the West Lake section's Dunes Day-Use area, consists of a sandy bay surrounded by enormous dunes. The drop-off here occurs closer to shore than it does at the other two beaches, and although it is marked with buoys, swimmers should exercise caution when venturing beyond them.

Between Outlet and Sandbanks Beach is West Point. Limestone cliffs lead down to the shoreline and provide shelter for the point's many swallows. Due to the powerful undertow offshore, swimming is not allowed, but it is a great place to escape the beach crowds and explore a different terrain, including the ruins of Lakeshore Lodge, with its tennis court, shuffleboard area and the remains of a terrazzo dance floor. In August, park staff don costumes from the late 1800s and host a Lakeshore Lodge Day, complete with tug-of-war, potato-sack and three-legged races and a rolling-pin toss.

Park trails allow visitors to experience the dune and wetland habitats. The 3.5-kilometre (2.2 mi) Woodlands Trail starts at the Main Gate parking lot and continues through the Woodland Campground, farm pastures and hardwood lots until it reaches the Dunes Day-Use area. The two-kilometre (1.2 mi) Cedar Sands Nature Trail loop — an interpretive trail with 12 stops — runs along the shores of the Outlet River. Two lookouts offer scenic views of the marsh. The 2.5-kilometre (1.6 mi) Sandbanks Dunes Trail loop travels through fragile dune habitat and along the edge of several rare wetland habitats called pannes.

Sandbanks is another important location on Lake Ontario during bird migration in spring and fall, and the park is known for its plentiful numbers of wild turkeys, raccoons, skunks and white-tailed deer.

Sandbanks has over 500 car campsites and two group campsites that can accommodate 30 to 50 people. There are also two cottages: Maplerest Heritage House, a four-bedroom Victorian with antiques, sleeps eight; Jacques Cottage, a one-and-a-half storey, sleeps six.

Things to See & Do

- Build sandcastles in the warm, golden sand.
- Hike the three distinctly different trails.
- Try kite boarding or windsurfing.
- Watch for wildlife, including wild turkeys and white-tailed deer.

Sandbanks Provincial Park
3004 County Road 12 RR 1
Picton, ON K0K 2T0
613-393-3319
ontarioparks.com/park/ sandbanks
friendsofsandbanks.org/ site/home

66

THE COUNTY
~ Prince Edward County

Prince Edward County — regionally known as The County — is technically an island, surrounded on the north and east by the Bay of Quinte, with the Murray Canal connecting the bay to Lake Ontario across the only land connection. It encompasses roughly 100,000 hectares (247,105 acres), with almost 800 kilometres (497 mi) of Lake Ontario shoreline.

Although settled some 2,000 years ago by Indigenous peoples — The County has many important archaeological sites — Upper Canada's founding lieutenant-governor, John Graves Simcoe, named it for Prince Edward Augustus (fourth son of King George III), commander-in-chief of British North America, and the Crown granted land in the area to some of the earliest United Empire Loyalists to encourage their settlement in Ontario.

The Loyalist Parkway (Highway 33) follows a colonial pioneer route through the island, connecting several historical settlement sites, as well as 40 archaeological sites and around 125 heritage buildings. Picton and Milford both offer heritage walking tours, and The County is home to five museums, six lighthouses, a pioneer village and a life-sized bronze sculpture of former resident Sir John A. Macdonald.

A mild climate and limestone-rich soil have helped make Prince Edward County the fastest-growing wine region in Canada.

ABOVE, LEFT AND RIGHT: Lake on the Mountain is located nearly 62 metres (203 ft) above the Bay of Quinte, separated by a narrow strip of land that ends in a cliff; this view shows the elevation of the lake. LEFT: Despite a growing population and a healthy influx of tourism, The County maintains its slower rural pace.

Things to See & Do

- Discover the many historic stops along the Loyalist Parkway.
- Hike the diverse topography of the Millennium Trail.
- Visit mysterious Lake on the Mountain.
- Attend one of The County's many festivals.

Prince Edward County Chamber of Tourism and Commerce
116 Main Street
Picton, ON K0K 2T0
613-476-2421
business.pecchamber. com
visitpec.ca
prince-edward-county.com

The County has long been known for its working farms, picturesque vineyards and overall pastoral scenery, but it also offers visitors a compelling range of destinations and activities: parks, conservation areas, sand and pebble beaches, nature trails, walking circles, unique shopping experiences, golf courses, music festivals, theatre, birding festivals, waterfall tours and year-round fishing. The Bay of Quinte is known as "Walleye Capital of the World," in summer waters as well as through a thick layer of ice.

The County's Millennium Trail system covers about 73.5 hectares (182 acres), starting in Carrying Place and winding its way to Picton through diverse natural landscapes — farm fields, forests, marshes and creeks.

A popular natural attraction is mysterious Lake on the Mountain. This freshwater lake is located nearly 62 metres (203 ft) above the Bay of Quinte, separated by a narrow strip of land that ends in a cliff. The lake appears to have no source of fresh water, and early settlers believed it to be bottomless. (In truth, it is approximately 34 metres (112 ft) deep and fed by seasonal streams and a nearby swamp.) Another highlight, Sandbanks Provincial Park, appears earlier, in chapter 65.

The County keeps busy, and each month brings a fresh list of events, so keep an eye on its website. September alone features performances by the renowned Festival Players; Women Killing It, a female crime writers' festival; Red, White & Blues, a festival of wine and blues music; the Picton Fall Fair; the Prince Edward County (Classical) Music Festival; the Sandbanks (Indie) Music Festival; the Live '50s & '60s Rock'n'Roll Festival; the Prince Edward County Studio & Gallery Tour; and the TASTE Community Grown Festival, showcasing The County's food producers, restaurants, wineries and cideries.

67

THOUSAND ISLANDS NATIONAL PARK
～ St. Lawrence River

Accessible from the Thousand Islands Parkway, Thousand Islands National Park promotes sustainable recreation while protecting the land and wildlife that make the area a popular tourist destination. Established in 1904, it was the first Canadian national park east of the Rockies.

Thousand Islands National Park includes several ecologically important mainland sites and more than 20 islands located between Kingston and Brockville.

LEFT: An osprey fishing one of the channels through the islands in Thousand Islands National Park. BELOW: One of many small harbours in this boater's paradise. FACING PAGE: An aerial view of the Thousand Islands International Bridge connecting Canada and the United States across the St. Lawrence River.

The Visitor Centre at Mallory-town Landing is a good place to start your adventure.

The two trails that launch at Mallorytown Landing — Six Nations Trail and Smoky Fire Trail (with the Loyalist Trail loop as an option) — are relatively easy: All three can be comfortably completed in about 90 minutes. Another trail network can be accessed via Landon Bay, where a number of well-posted trail information signs lead visitors through forests, fields and wetlands. True to its name, Lookout Trail offers one of the best views in the Thousand Islands region. The trails at Jones Creek are rugged but family-friendly. Spend as little as 20 minutes on the shorter trails or take a whole day to hike the six trails that wind through the park.

If wildlife viewing is on your wish list, Thousand Islands National Park is an excellent place to encounter osprey, great blue herons, map turtles, mink and white-tailed deer. Coyotes, foxes, porcupines, beaver and weasels are also at home here. The early-morning hours and just before dusk are typically the best times to spot animals.

The park has 27 campsites that can be reserved in advance, as well as 34 first-come, first-served campsites. Parks Canada now offers oTENTik camping. Accommodation that is a cross between a tent and a rustic cabin, oTENTik camping is available on McDonald Island and Gordon Island, and five oTENTik tents are available on the mainland at Mallorytown Landing.

One of the more rewarding ways to explore Thousand Islands National Park is by kayak. Bring your own or rent from numerous regional outfitters. And with its countless shoals, the region also boasts some of the best scuba-diving in Ontario. Many a ship found its final resting place in these waters. A number of dive charter companies provide guided tours of the islands' sunken history.

Things to See & Do

- Explore the park's trails and lookouts.
- View the region's abundant wildlife.
- Experience oTENTik camping.
- Scuba-dive among the shipwrecks.

Thousand Islands National Park
2 County Road 5, RR 3
Mallorytown, ON
K0E 1R0
613-923-5261
pc.gc.ca/eng/pn-np/on/lawren/index.aspx

68 UPPER CANADA VILLAGE
∿ Morrisburg

Upper Canada Village is the legacy of a heritage preservation plan implemented in 1958 when the building of the St. Lawrence Seaway necessitated the flooding of 10 small communities. Heritage buildings of all descriptions were relocated to a site owned by the St. Lawrence Parks Commission, and Upper Canada Village was assembled to portray daily life in an English-Canadian village in the year 1866.

From May through September, authentically costumed re-enactors of all ages bring to life a fully functioning 19th-century village. The more than 40 historic buildings include an operational sawmill and flour mill; a woollen mill and a textile factory; a cheese factory, a bakery and a dry goods store; a weaver, a dressmaker and a shoemaker; a tinsmith, a blacksmith and a broom-maker; a cooper and a cabinetmaker; a progressive farm, a traditional farm and a tenant farm; an Anglican

Things to See & Do

- Discover how life was lived in Ontario circa 1866.
- Tour the village in costume and have your photo taken.
- Take a 20-minute wagon ride.
- Travel the village canal via horse-drawn tow scow.

Upper Canada Village
13740 County Road 2
Morrisburg, ON
K0C 1X0
613-543-4328
1-800-437-2233
uppercanadavillage.com

church, an Episcopal Methodist chapel and a Lutheran pastor's house; an engine house with a hand-pump fire engine; a schoolhouse and a community centre; a newspaper office and a physician's home; and, of course, a tavern and a hotel. Each business, trade and profession is recreated in pleasing and painstaking detail.

An audio-visual presentation in Crysler Hall, the home of a prosperous landowner, helps orient visitors to life in the mid-1860s. You can even role-play by booking an appointment with the Costume Studio, where you will be outfitted in period attire for your stroll around the village. In July and August, children visiting the Family Activity Centre can participate in 19th-century crafts and games. Willard's Hotel offers traditional meals served by costumed staff.

A scaled replica of a C. P. Huntington locomotive named *The Moccasin* travels along the river through Crysler Heritage Park, and the story of the Battle of Crysler's Farm is broadcast along the way. Admission to the park is free, and visitors are invited to view an interactive battlefield model and theatre-of-war map explaining the strategies and struggles behind the bloody conflict that took place on November 11, 1813.

Finally, visitors can experience the village aboard the horse-drawn tow scow. The scow seats 60 and is poled along the canal from the dock behind Cook's Tavern to the village's tenant farm.

ABOVE: Re-enactors bring to life a fully functioning 19th-century village. Here, a carpenter plies his trade. Visitors will also meet blacksmiths, tinsmiths, coopers, millers, weavers, dressmakers, shoemakers, farmers, and more. FACING PAGE: Christ Church Anglican was built in 1837. The church has a fine reed organ built in 1862 by Samuel Warren of Montreal. The interior contains no cross and no altar candles, as such things were unacceptable to this congregation in the 1860s.

69

BYWARD MARKET
~ Ottawa

ByWard Market is Canada's oldest continuously operating farmers' market and one of the largest.

With more than 600 storefront businesses and over 260 stands devoted to the harvest of local farmers and the work of local artisans, the ByWard Market is one of the country's oldest and largest public markets. It's also considered Ottawa's number-one tourist attraction: Some 50,000 visitors flock to this four-block area on summer weekends, and an estimated 10 million pass through in a given year.

Designated a Heritage Conservation District, the market area of historic Lower Town has retained much of its Victorian charm. In an era of suburbanization and shopping malls, the ByWard Market continues to be a vital centre of social activity and commerce. A recent count of businesses tallied 109 restaurants, 22 retail food outlets, 24 nightclubs and entertainment venues, 48 fashion shops,

LEFT: The market is a focus for city events. Here, the mechanized spectacle "La Machine" makes an appearance in July 2017. BELOW LEFT: The Chateau Lafayette on York Street in the ByWard Market was established in 1849 and is the oldest tavern in Ottawa. BELOW RIGHT: A ByWard Market vendor sells maple syrup in all forms and formats.

Things to See & Do

- Experience the fresh food and vibrant market atmosphere.
- See how history meets high-end shopping.
- Enjoy diverse busker performances.
- Savour some of the 100 plus dining options.

ByWard Market
55 ByWard Market
  Square
Ottawa, ON K1N 9C3
613-562-3325
byward-market.com

29 other boutiques, 39 health-related stores and beauty salons, 12 houseware shops, 14 galleries and arts facilities, seven bookstores and news shops and 45 professional offices.

The market was established during Lieutenant-Colonel John By's 1826 survey of the community that would briefly bear his name (Bytown). The engineer who famously supervised construction of the Rideau Canal first had to construct a town to house his workers and their families. In By's street plan for the market district, George Street and York Street were to be 132 feet wide (40 m) to allow for a courthouse, a market building and street commerce.

The Market Square building houses Moulin de Provence, renowned for its authentic patisserie and tourtière. Across the street, the House of Cheese offers prize-winning Ontario cheeses and poutine-worthy cheese curds. Nearby, Stubbe Chocolates creates handmade truffles, chocolate bars and traditional stollen.

The ByWard Market district is also home to the National Gallery of Canada, Notre Dame Basilica and the Chateau Lafayette, which opened in 1849 and remains Ottawa's oldest tavern.

70

CANADA DAY
ON PARLIAMENT HILL
~ Ottawa

FACING PAGE: Fireworks explode in the night sky above Canada's Parliament Buildings as part of the country's birthday celebrations. Crowds of over 300,000 gather at well-chosen locations to enjoy the best fireworks of the year.

Things to See & Do

- Hear top performers on the Parliament Hill stage.
- Watch the Snowbirds and the RCMP Musical Ride.
- Enjoy free museum and gallery admission.
- Take in the grand fireworks celebration.

Canada Day Hotline
1-844-878-8333
canadaday.gc.ca

Parliament of Canada
Ottawa, ON K1A 0A9
1-866-599-4999
613-992-4793

Every Canadian should try to attend at least one Canada Day celebration in the nation's capital. The collective spirit is electric, and the patriotic wave that swells through the crowd is decidedly more thankful than boastful. Ours is a great country.

You can observe the Canada Day parade along Elgin Street from a prime spot in Gatineau Park, take part in the multicultural activities at the World Pavilion in Rideau Falls Park, witness the changing of the guard, watch the RCMP musical ride, then look up to the sky as the famous Snowbirds fly in formation overhead. You can tour Rideau Hall and visit museums and other attractions for free. Entertainment on the Parliament Hill main stage continues throughout the day as performers from every province and territory delight the thousands of Canadians gathered family-picnic-style on the vast lawn.

Experiencing Canada Day on Parliament Hill is a smile-inducing reminder that Canadians' legendary politeness and orderliness makes it possible to stand just an arm's length from the Prime Minister on July 1, to meet and speak to the Governor-General, to rub shoulders with our country's most famous politicians, scientists, athletes, writers, musicians, actors and other public personalities as we all celebrate together.

Around 10 p.m., be sure to find a comfortable spot to watch the spectacular fireworks as they rise above the Ottawa River, fill the sky and frame the Peace Tower. Crowds of over 300,000 gather at key locations such as Major's Hill Park and Jacques-Cartier Park to watch the year's grandest fireworks exhibition.

Touring the Parliament Buildings, you'll learn that construction of the Centre, East and West blocks commenced in 1859 and finished in 1866, just one year before Confederation. On February 3, 1916, a fire that started in the Commons reading room, in the Centre Block, claimed seven lives and destroyed all but the northwest wing and the library. Reconstruction of the Modern Gothic Revival-style Centre Block was completed in 1922. The Peace Tower was completed in 1927.

The red-and-gold-themed Senate Chamber is found at the east end of the Centre Block. The House of Commons Chamber, at the west end, is decorated in green, in the manner of the British House of Commons. Between the House and the Senate are Confederation Hall and the Hall of Honour; at the end of the Hall is the Library of Parliament. The domed, circular Victorian Gothic Revival-style Library has at its centre a white marble statue of young Queen Victoria.

The 93-metre (305 ft) Peace Tower honours those Canadians who died in armed conflicts and commemorates Canada's commitment to peace. ~

71 CANADIAN MUSEUM OF NATURE
～ Ottawa

The Canadian Museum of Nature's main collections were started by the Geological Survey of Canada in 1856 and have since grown to include more than 14.6 million mineralogical, paleontological, zoological and botanical specimens.

The museum is housed in Ottawa's grand Victoria Memorial Museum Building, a massive stone structure designed by David Ewart, the architect of many similar structures around the city. Inspired by Hampton Court and Windsor Castle, its architectural style has been described as Scottish baronial. In fact, 300 Scottish stonemasons were involved in its construction. In 1990, the building was designated a National Historic Site.

The museum grounds are themselves an exhibit. The Landscapes of Canada Gardens contain approximately 60 species of native plants and trees from the prairie grasslands, the boreal forest and the Arctic tundra. The gardens also feature a 13-metre-high (43 ft) steel iceberg sculpture and a romping family of mammoths.

Inside are eight permanent exhibition galleries. The Fossil Gallery contains skeletons of dinosaurs and ancient marine reptiles. Almost 85 percent of the specimens on display are genuine fossils, as opposed to fabrications or casts. Visitors can see more than 30 complete skeletons from the end of the dinosaur era (85 to 65 million years ago), as well as 15 life-sized models. Among the newest acquisitions is *Spiclypeus shipporum*, a horned dinosaur that lived 76 million years ago.

The Earth Gallery is filled with rocks and minerals and reveals how geological forces have shaped our planet. Among the highlights is the indoor limestone cave complete with stalactites, stalagmites and trickling water.

The Water Gallery contains exhibits about marine and freshwater environments and the critical role that water plays in sustaining all living things. There are plenty of live specimens, but the star of the gallery is the complete skeleton of a blue whale — the largest animal on Earth.

Nature Live offers encounters with live insects, arachnids and slugs, beetles,

RIGHT: Housed in a century-old national historic heritage building, the Canadian Museum of Nature features world-class galleries and interactive programming.

Things to See & Do

- Meet the mammoth family on the museum grounds.
- Examine the many dinosaur skeletons in the Fossil Gallery.
- Marvel at the enormous blue whale skeleton.
- Check out the 450 species of mounted birds.

Canadian Museum
  of Nature
240 McLeod Street
Victoria Memorial
  Museum Building
Ottawa, ON
K2P 2R1
613-566-4700
1-800-263-4433
nature.ca/en/home

honeybees, stick insects, tarantulas, hissing cockroaches and many other delightful creatures.

Canada's wild animals occupy the Mammal Gallery, including mounted grizzly bears, polar bears, bison, moose, caribou, pronghorns and cougars. Discover the ways they have adapted to survive in Canada. Meanwhile, the Bird Gallery features nearly 500 mounts of 450 species of Canadian birds, allowing visitors to examine their delicate beauty at close range. You can try to match a bird to its song, identify species and imitate bird calls. In a special area of the gallery, visitors learn about taking care of injured birds.

The Stone Wall Gallery is a space for art and photography about natural science, including flora of the Canadian Arctic.

The Canada Goose Arctic Gallery, a new permanent gallery, seeks to enhance and transform our understanding of the Arctic and its importance to Canada. It's a great place to learn about the region's geography, ecosystems and sustainability, as well as the impacts of climate change.

72

CANADIAN TULIP FESTIVAL

∼ Ottawa

The Canadian Tulip Festival, held annually in Ottawa over three May weekends, holds the title for "world's largest tulip festival," displaying as many as three million tulips for the enjoyment of city residents and the more than 500,000 visitors who attend the festival.

It all began in 1945, when the Dutch royal family sent 100,000 tulip bulbs to Ottawa to express their gratitude to Canadians for having sheltered Dutch Princess Juliana and her daughters during the three-year Nazi occupation of the Netherlands. In 1946, Juliana herself sent another 20,500 bulbs with the request that a display be created for Ottawa Civic Hospital, where she had given birth to Princess Margriet in 1943. She promised to send 10,000 more bulbs each year thereafter.

Of course, Ottawa soon became famous for its tulips, and in 1953, the Ottawa Board of Trade and photographer Malak Karsh organized the first Canadian Tulip Festival. The Netherlands continues to send 20,000 bulbs to Canada each year — 10,000 from the royal family and 10,000 from the Dutch Bulb Growers Association. Today, nearly three million bulbs are purchased from Dutch and Canadian distributors. The late Malak Karsh became widely known for his Tulip Festival photographs and for transforming Ottawa's sombre image.

The largest display is found in

Things to See & Do

- Visit the vast display at Commissioners Park.
- Take a Garden Promenade tour.
- Discover the tulip art in ByWard Market.
- Participate in multicultural activities in Major's Hill Park.

Canadian Tulip
  Festival Inc.
The Horticulture
  Building
203–1525 Princess
  Patricia Way
Ottawa, ON K1S 5J3
1-800-668-8547
tulipfestival.ca

LEFT: Some of the remarkable tulips that bloom at the "world's largest tulip festival," which boasts up to three million tulips during this annual event. BELOW: Everyone participates in the downtown Tulip Festival spirit.

ABOVE: The Ottawa Tulip Festival under blue skies with the Parliament buildings in the background. FACING PAGE: Major's Hill Park during Tulip Festival, with the library of Parliament as a backdrop.

Commissioners Park, along the shores of Dow's Lake, where visitors can see over 300,000 individual tulips from 60 different varieties. Commissioners Park also features buskers, musicians and artists throughout the festival.

At Major's Hill Park, the tented International Pavilion features food and entertainment from various diverse cultures, while several embassies and local community groups host crafts and activities for children. Lansdowne Park Tulip Gallery teems with tulip art and floral exhibits, artistic installations and interactive family programming and entertainment.

At ByWard Tulip PARK(ing), pop artist Bex, creator of the festival's "One Tulip One Canada" flag, brings stylized tulip art to the city's central marketplace, with massive art installations on the City Parkade and artist-led workshops.

Finally, the Garden Promenade celebrates Ottawa's garden culture with more than 70 experiences and access to 40 of the region's most beautiful gardens. Join an escorted tour of Ottawa's public gardens or pick up a self-guided tour map.

73

RIDEAU CANAL
NATIONAL HISTORIC SITE
∿ Ottawa–Kingston

The Rideau Canal was completed in 1832 to forge a water route from Montreal to Kingston and Lake Ontario, avoiding both the rapids and the threat from United States forces along the St. Lawrence River. Here, the canal joins the Ottawa River.

The historic Rideau Canal makes its way south from Ottawa, its 19th-century locks linking rivers and lakes via manmade channels for 202 kilometres (126 mi) before reaching Kingston and Lake Ontario.

Construction of the canal began in 1826, with memories of the War of 1812 still fresh on the minds of politicians and citizenry. In the event of another American invasion, the waterway would ensure military and commercial supply routes. The canal was completed in 1832 — a monumental feat of engineering and human labour — but the feared American invasion didn't happen. Today, the

American flags seen along the canal are attached to the boats of welcome tourists.

Built under the direction of Lieutenant-Colonel John By of the British Corps of Royal Engineers, the Rideau Canal system comprises 47 locks, 24 lock stations and the watersheds of the Rideau and the Cataraqui rivers. A lesser-known fact is that only 19 kilometres (12 mi) of the system is cut channel. Indigenous peoples travelled the lakes and rivers of the Rideau waterway route for centuries before the canal system was undertaken. The Rideau system continues to offer an abundance of natural paddling environments — lakes, rivers and wetlands. The best time to paddle is during spring and fall (cooler temperatures, fewer powerboaters).

Housed in a 19th-century stone mill, the Rideau Canal Visitor Centre in Smiths Falls is the system's main interpretation centre, with three floors of exhibits and a 15-minute video presentation that explains the construction and operation of the historic canal, as well as how it became a National Historic Site of Canada, a designated Canadian Heritage River and a UNESCO World Heritage Site.

The Rideau Canal is accessible by road, bicycle and hiking trails and, of course, canoe, kayak and boat. Many of its 24 lock stations offer self-guided

Lock stations no. 1–8 at the Rideau Canal waterway, with the Fairmont Chateau Laurier Hotel in the background.

Things to See & Do

- Visit the Rideau Canal Visitor Centre in Smiths Falls.
- See the lockmaster hand-crank the locks just as it was done in 1832.
- Paddle or boat a canal section, lock to lock.
- Rent a houseboat and make the canal your summer-holiday destination.

Rideau Canal
 Visitor Centre
34 Beckwith St. South
Smiths Falls, ON
K7A 2A8
613-283-5170
pc.gc.ca/en/lhn-nhs/
 on/rideau

walking tours in historic settings. This is Old Ontario, and well-preserved 19th-century towns and military posts abound. It is living history to watch the lockmaster hand-crank winches to open and close the massive lock gates.

Given the system's more than 1,000 kilometres (620 mi) of shoreline, visitors can pick a destination for a day trip, paddle and camp for a week or travel the canal's entire length. If you don't own your own watercraft, you have your choice of renting everything from kayaks to houseboats.

There are many places to stop for a swim or relax on a sandy beach, and fishing along the canal is always popular, with opportunities for largemouth and smallmouth bass, yellow perch, walleye, lake trout, northern pike and even muskellunge.

All lock stations except the Ottawa locks and Smith Falls Combined Locks offer well-serviced campsites for a low fee. Boaters who pay for overnight mooring can camp for free. ∾

FACING PAGE: Displays at the Rideau Canal Visitor Centre in Smiths Falls tell the story of the historic canal.
ABOVE: Winter on the Rideau Canal with the Chateau Laurier in the background.

74

WINTERLUDE
～ Ottawa

Learning to embrace winter is part of being Canadian, and each February, the Department of Canadian Heritage brings that philosophy to a whole new level. For three straight weekends, Winterlude celebrations take over downtown Ottawa and Gatineau, Quebec, the city across the river, where the festival is known as *le Bal de Neige*.

The Winterlude Kick-Off party takes place in Confederation Park, usually on the first Friday in February, and features live performances as well as DJ'd music and a dance-party light show. Like most Winterlude events, this party is free to the public.

The Rideau Canal Skateway is the setting for many of the festival's events. At 7.8 kilometres (5 mi) in length, the Skateway is often referred to as "the largest skating rink in the world." Bring your own skates or rent a pair on site. If you tire of the Skateway, there's also the Rink of Dreams at Marion Dewar Plaza, outside City Hall, which hosts skating shows, dance events and interactive art displays.

North America's only Ice Dragon Boat Festival is also held on the Skateway, with competitors propelling their colourful, streamlined iceboats with poles rather than paddles. The annual Accora Village Bed Race sees 50 costumed teams, each comprising four "pushers" and one rider, drive elaborately decorated hospital beds down the ice to raise money for Kiwanis Club charities.

Artists from around the world fill Confederation Park for the Crystal Garden International Ice-Carving Competition, where professional carvers transform

BELOW LEFT: Ice sculptors take part in the Winterlude festival contest at Confederation Park. BELOW RIGHT: An ice sculpture of a surfer is illuminated at a night-time Winterlude event in Confederation Park.

ABOVE: People enjoying Winterlude on the "largest outdoor skating rink in the world." BELOW: Warming up with hot chocolate and BeaverTails at Confederation Park, a much-loved Winterlude ritual.

blocks of ice into magnificent sculptures before your eyes. The Crystal Garden also hosts the Sub-Zero Concert Series throughout the festival.

If all of this skating and racing and carving makes you hungry and thirsty, you'll appreciate the spectrum of culinary options, including walkabout winter feasts, chef demonstrations at local restaurants, the Winter BrewFest, the ByWard Market's Annual Winterlude Stew Cook-Off and perhaps a trip (or two) to the Grand Outdoor Ice Bar.

And while it's not on the Ontario side of the river, parents should know that downtown Gatineau's Jacques Cartier Park is home to a giant children's snow playground called the Snowflake Kingdom for the duration of Winterlude/ *le Bal de Neige*. It's a great place for kids to encounter the festival mascots, the Ice Hogs (cheery and cheerily dressed groundhogs).

Things to See & Do

- Skate on the Rideau Skateway.
- Witness the results of the International Ice-Carving Competition.
- Attend free concerts in Confederation Park.
- Experience the Stew Cook-Off and Outdoor Ice Bar.

Winterlude Visitor Info
1-844-878-8333
ottawatourism.ca/
ottawa-insider/
winterlude

187

COTTAGE COUNTRY
& NORTHERN
ONTARIO

75 ⌁ Agawa Canyon Train Tour   Sault Ste. Marie

76 ⌁ Algonquin Provincial Park & Barron Canyon
      Algonquin Provincial Park

77 ⌁ Beausoleil Island   Port Severn

78 ⌁ Big Nickel, Dynamic Earth & Science North
      Sudbury

79 ⌁ Canadian Canoe Museum   Peterborough

80 ⌁ Cross-Country Skiing in Muskoka   Muskoka

81 ⌁ Fathom Five National Marine Park
      & Flowerpot Island   Tobermory

82 ⌁ French River Provincial Park   Alban

83 ⌁ Haliburton Sculpture Forest   Haliburton

84 ⌁ Ice Fishing on Lake Simcoe   Lake Simcoe

85 ⌁ Killarney Provincial Park
      & the La Cloche Mountains   Killarney

86 ⌁ Manitoulin Island Indigenous Adventures
      Manitoulin Island

87 ⌁ Mariposa Folk Festival   Orillia

88 ⌁ "Mineral Capital of Canada"   Bancroft

89 ⌁ Moose Safaris & Wolf Howls   Algonquin
      Provincial Park

90 ⌁ Muskoka Steamships & Discovery Centre
      Gravenhurst

91 ⌁ Paddlepalooza Kayak Festival   Parry Sound

92 ⌁ Petroglyphs Provincial Park & National
      Historic Site   Woodview/Peterborough

93 ⌁ Sainte-Marie Among the Hurons
      National Historic Site   Midland

94 ⌁ Trent–Severn Waterway
      & Peterborough Lift Lock National Historic
      Site   Trenton–Peterborough–Port Severn

95 ⌁ Wasaga Beach Provincial Park
      Wasaga Beach

NORTHERN ONTARIO

96 ⌁ Kakabeka Falls   Kakabeka Falls

97 ⌁ Polar Bear Provincial Park   Hudson Bay

98 ⌁ Sleeping Giant Provincial Park
      & Ouimet Canyon   Pass Lake

99 ⌁ Terry Fox Memorial & Lookout
      Thunder Bay

100 ⌁ Wabakimi Provincial Park
       Armstrong Station

1

Polar Bear Provincial Park

Hudson Bay

NUNAVUT

ONTARIO

97

2

Sault Ste. Marie
75
17

Elliot Lake

Thessalon

Spanish

144
Sudbury
78
Nickel Centre

17
Walden

Verner

Alban

82

Quebec

17

Algonquin Provincial Park
76

89

86
85
Killarney

Manitowaning

Lake Huron

ONTARIO
U.S.A.

Georgian Bay

Parry Sound
91

69

11

11

11

Tobermory 81

3

Wabakimi Provincial Park
100

527
Lake Nipigon

11

Sleeping Giant Provincial Park

17

11
Kakabeka Falls
Thunder Bay
96
99
98

17

.S.A.

Lake Superior

4

400

11

Georgian Bay

Haliburton 83

Bancroft 88

80
90
Gravenhurst

28

77
93
Midland

87
Orillia

92
Woodview

95
Wasaga Beach

Lake Simcoe

84

26

7

79
94
Peterborough

12

89

9

400
404
407
401

Lake Ontario

75

AGAWA CANYON TRAIN TOUR
~ Sault Ste. Marie

Things to See & Do

- Experience the rugged northern landscape in true comfort.
- Hike the canyon's rim and thrill to four waterfalls.
- Visit the Canadian Bushplane Heritage Centre.

Agawa Canyon
  Train Tour
Algoma Central Railway
129 Bay Street
Sault Ste. Marie, ON
P6A 6Y2
705-946-7300
1-800-242-9287
agawatrain.com

Canadian Bushplane
  Heritage Centre
50 Pim Street
Sault Ste. Marie, ON
P6A 3G4
705-945-6242
1-877-287-4752
bushplane.com

Located 183 kilometres (114 mi) northwest of Sault Ste. Marie, Agawa Canyon Wilderness Park is accessible only by hiking trail or via the historic Algoma Central Railway. Of course, the best way to experience the vast beauty of this northern landscape is to take the train *to* the trails.

The Agawa Canyon Train Tour is a distinctly memorable 10-hour round-trip excursion from Sault Ste. Marie, available daily from mid-June to mid-October. The comfortable, well-appointed train features a GPS-activated commentary, available in five languages (English, French, German, Japanese and Mandarin), that alerts passengers to points of interest along the way and shares stories of the region's Ojibwe people, early explorers and fur traders.

Digital cameras mounted on the locomotive stream the engineer's view to flat-screen monitors installed throughout the coaches, though screens are no match for what's on offer through the train's large windows as the inspiringly rugged landscape rolls by. Group of Seven members Lawren Harris, A. Y. Jackson, Frank Johnston, A. E. H. MacDonald and Arthur Lismer were so captivated by Agawa's beauty that between 1918 and 1923, they travelled to the region aboard a specially outfitted Algoma Central boxcar.

The bedrock beneath the canyon is part of the Canadian Shield, among the oldest rock on Earth. The canyon was created as the result of faulting more than a billion years ago. Its walls reach 175 metres (575 ft) at their highest point, and four waterfalls spill into the Agawa River from the rim of the canyon: Otter Creek Falls, North Black Beaver Falls, South Black Beaver Falls and the highest, Bridal Veil Falls, at 68.5 metres (225 ft).

The train enters the canyon at mile 102 and over the next 16 kilometres (10 mi) descends 152 metres (500 ft) to the canyon floor. At mile 114, passengers disembark to experience the canyon up close via one or more of the five short nature trails. Some trails lead to the waterfalls. Another option is the 350-stair climb to the Lookout, 76 metres (250 ft) above the canyon floor.

A number of affordable train tours are offered throughout the year, including a popular Fall Colours Tour and a winter Snow Train Tour. A three-night package, with accommodation in the Sault, has several perks and passes, including entry to the Canadian Bushplane Heritage Centre, which features more than 25 historic aircraft. ~

LEFT: The Agawa train chugs through a landscape once travelled by Ojibwe, fur traders and explorers. FACING PAGE: At its highest point, the Agawa Canyon plunges some 175 metres (575 ft) to the Agawa River.

76 ALGONQUIN PROVINCIAL PARK & BARRON CANYON

∼ Algonquin Provincial Park

Due to its relative accessibility to southern Ontario's urban population, Algonquin Park is an extraordinarily popular place in peak summer, so I recommend an autumn visit. Situated in the transition zone between southern deciduous forests and northern coniferous forests, the park vibrates with intense colour in the fall. That said, Algonquin is large enough that anyone willing to spend a day paddling and portaging into the interior lakes can experience a sense of wilderness even in peak season.

The best way to explore Algonquin Park is by canoe. The park features over 2,000 kilometres (1,243 mi) of paddling possibilities, with routes suited to paddlers at all skill levels. A weekend spent paddling the outer lakes can be rejuvenating. A week or more spent exploring the interior lakes can be life-changing.

The Barron River Canyon can be explored via canoe or by hiking the loop trail along its northern rim.

Although Algonquin is renowned for its network of waterways, its majestic maple hills and rugged granite ridges can also be accessed on foot. Fourteen hiking trails head out from eight campgrounds located along a 56-kilometre (35 mi) stretch of Highway 60 that runs through the south end of the park.

Located on the eastern boundary of Algonquin Park, the spectacular 100-metre-deep (328 ft) Barron Canyon was cut by the precursor of today's Barron River, a waterway that, at the end of the last ice age, carried the outflow from massive Lake Agassiz (from which the Great Lakes developed).

The 1.5-kilometre (1 mi) Barron Canyon loop trail will take you along the northern rim for some amazing views before leading you back to the parking lot. The canyon can also be explored by canoe, with access points at the Brigham Lake parking lot and the Barron River parking lot.

Things to See & Do

- Experience Ontario's near wilderness in its autumn colours.
- Explore Algonquin Park's rivers and lakes via canoe.
- Hike the spectacular Barron Canyon loop trail.

Algonquin Provincial Park
Highway 60
P.O. Box 219
Whitney, ON K0J 2M0
705-633-5572
ontarioparks.com/park/
  algonquin
algonquinpark.on.ca
  (The Friends of
  Algonquin Park)

FACING PAGE AND ABOVE: Algonquin Park features more than 2,000 kilometres (1,243 mi) of paddling possibilities. RIGHT: Highway 60 winds its way across the southern part of the park, with access to trails, campgrounds and outfitters. FOLLOWING PAGES: The park in magnificent autumn colour.

77 BEAUSOLEIL ISLAND
~ Port Severn

Beausoleil Island is served by the Parks Canada shuttle boat *DayTripper*. Hikers and cyclists can experience the island's northern wetlands, granite out-crops and southern beaches via 12 trails.

At eight kilometres (5 mi) long, Beausoleil Island is the largest island in Lake Huron's Georgian Bay Islands National Park. Unless you are operating your own boat, Beausoleil is accessed via the Parks Canada shuttle boat, the *DayTripper*, from Honey Harbour, a 15-minute trip. Biking is a great way to see more of the island, and depending on available space, visitors are invited to bring their bicycles aboard. Alternatively, bikes can be rented at the Cedar Spring Visitor Centre on the island.

The Huron, Christian and Georgian trails are open for cycling. The Huron and Christian trails wind through mature forest at relatively easy grade, while the rugged Georgian trail attracts the more seasoned cyclist. These three trails access most other trails in the park, so many visitors plan combined bike-and-hike excursions.

Northern Beausoleil hiking trails offer the park's best views of Georgian Bay's iconic Canadian Shield landscape — massive mounds of exposed granite, tena-cious windswept pines and vast stretches of clear blue water. But the northern region also features a wetland habitat in which many creatures thrive, includ-ing diverse species of birds, small mammals, amphibians and reptiles. Beausoleil

Things to See & Do

- Hike 12 trails.
- Explore wooded trails by bicycle.
- Canoe or kayak the island's shoreline and bays.
- Watch for 33 reptile species.

Park Administrative Office
901 Wye Valley Road
P.O. Box 9
Midland, ON L4R 4K6
705-527-7200
1-888-773-8888
parkscanada.gc.ca/en/
pn-np/on/georg

Island is home to the threatened eastern Massasauga rattlesnake, Ontario's only poisonous snake. Don't worry, the Massasauga is small, has limited striking range, has no interest in humans and generally keeps its distance from hiking trails.

Southern Beausoleil's trails pass through a very different environment — mixed forests more characteristic of the west St. Lawrence Lowlands. Southern Beausoleil's Cedar Spring area hosts most of the park's camp and camping activities, including a welcome centre, cabin and oTENTik rentals, shoreline campsites, picnic shelters, swimming beaches, bike rentals and several easy trails.

On a historical note, artifacts as old as 7,000 years have been found on Beausoleil Island. Archaeologists believe the island was used as a summer camp by early hunter-gatherer cultures. Successive groups inhabited the land, notably the Point Peninsula and Saugeen peoples (2,400–1,300 years ago) and the Odawa (Ottawa) (600–400 years ago). Descendants of Lake Huron and Lake Simcoe Chippewa settled here in 1842. In 1856, Beausoleil and all other Georgian Bay islands were surrendered or sold to the Crown, with the exception of the Christian Islands, which were designated as a reserve. Chippewa residents of the Christian Islands still identify themselves as the Beausoleil First Nation.

78

BIG NICKEL, DYNAMIC EARTH & SCIENCE NORTH

∼ Sudbury

Things to See & Do

- Find the Big Nickel.
- Go seven storeys underground at Dynamic Earth.
- Think your way out of Science North's Escape Room.
- Travel to distant galaxies at the planetarium.

Dynamic Earth/
 The Big Nickel
122 Big Nickel Road
Sudbury, ON P3C 5T7
705-522-3701
1-800-461-4898
sciencenorth.ca/
 dynamic-earth

Science North
100 Ramsey Lake Road
Sudbury, ON
P3E 5S9
705-522-3701
1-800-461-4898
sciencenorth.ca

The mineral-rich Sudbury basin is believed to be a meteorite impact crater — one of the largest on Earth. By the early 20th century, Sudbury had become a major mining centre, extracting and processing one of the world's most valuable nickel deposits. But the impact of these activities had a devastating effect on the local environment. The already rugged, rocky landscape turned into a moonscape as sulphur dioxide and other airborne pollutants returned as acid rain, destroying forests and crops. The entire barren, blackened area was visible from space.

But at the beginning of the 1970s, when the International Nickel Company (INCO) built its 380-metre (1,250 ft) superstack chimney to disperse pollutants farther afield, Sudburians saw the opportunity to reclaim and reforest. Laurentian University and INCO worked with local volunteers — service clubs, scouts, school classes, citizen's groups, businesses and unemployed miners — to neutralize and fertilize the soil and to plant, one by one, more than 11 million trees. Sudbury's success in land reclamation has made it a world-recognized centre for environmental science issues relating to mining, and those interests are reflected in two of the city's prominent attractions, Dynamic Earth and Science North.

Dynamic Earth is home to the famous Big Nickel landmark. Sudbury resident Ted Szilva built the "largest coin in the world" in 1964, and it has been a roadside attraction ever since. The Big Nickel is a replica of a 1951 Canadian five-cent coin, except that it is 64,607,747 times the size of an actual Canadian nickel.

In the shadow of the Big Nickel is Dynamic Earth's Outdoor Science Park. Inside and out, the focus is on earth sciences, with compelling exhibits and plenty of hands-on activities for all ages. There are multimedia theatres, mineral and gemstone identification stations, earthquake displays and a guided tour that takes visitors seven storeys underground to experience the evolution of mining from the turn of the century to modern times.

Not far away is Science North, with its IMAX theatre, northern forest and wildlife labs, butterfly gallery, wetlands lab, cloud chamber, fossil exhibits, gravity well and much more. In Science North's Escape Room, players are locked in a room together and must solve a series of puzzles and crack codes to uncover clues in order to unlock the doors. A state-of-the-art planetarium features films about astronomy and other space topics projected on an 8.4-metre (27.5 ft) dome. The planetarium's use of the latest digital technologies takes visitors through near and distant galaxies, all the way to the outer reaches of the known universe. ∼

CLOCKWISE FROM LEFT:
Sudbury's famous Big Nickel,
the largest coin in the world;
young miners headed seven
storeys underground at
Dynamic Earth; inside the
Science North planetarium; an
aerial view of Science North.

79 CANADIAN CANOE MUSEUM
∼ Peterborough

For thousands of years, the canoe was essential to survival in this vast, watery land. More recently, in the 17th and 18th centuries, European explorers took up the canoe to push farther into the continent's interior. Many traders used canoes as primary transportation until the end of the 19th century.

With more than 600 canoes, kayaks and paddled watercraft — over 100 of which are on permanent display — the Canadian Canoe Museum seeks to explore "the canoe's enduring significance to the peoples of Canada."

The museum's collection is built upon the private collection of the late Kirk Wipper, a key figure in the development of outdoor education in Canada. A faculty member of the University of Toronto's School of Physical and Health Education, Wipper received a circa-1890 dugout canoe as a gift in 1957. Over the next decade, he acquired an additional 150 watercraft, which he kept

FACING PAGE: With more than 100 canoes on permanent display, the museum explores "the canoe's enduring significance to the peoples of Canada." LEFT: The museum's birch-bark winter wigwam, where you can listen to stories recorded by a Mi'kmaq elder. BELOW: A canoe used in the 1911 Coppermine Expedition to Great Bear Lake and the lower Coppermine River.

Things to See & Do

- Discover the importance of canoeing to Canada's history.
- Get a close-up look at over 100 paddled watercraft.
- Try to paddle as fast as a voyageur.
- Attend one of the museum's many programs and workshops.

Canadian Canoe
    Museum
910 Monaghan Road
Peterborough, ON
K9J 5K4
705-748-9153
1-866-342-2663
canoemuseum.ca

at Camp Kandalore, the summer camp he founded near Dorset. But his growing collection eventually led him to a search for a new facility. Thus, the Canadian Canoe Museum was established in Peterborough in 1997.

Among the museum's permanent collection are large dugouts built by First Nations people of the Pacific Northwest, bark canoes of Newfoundland's Beothuk, skin-on-frame kayaks from Baffin Island and all-wood and canvas-covered canoes from historic manufacturers such as Herald, Peterborough, Chestnut and Lakefield. International watercraft have been obtained from as far away as the Amazon.

The Canoe Museum engages with the broader community through family and school visits, adult canoeing programs and youth paddling camps, changing exhibits and special events. Younger visitors can participate in interactive hands-on galleries, build model canoes and enjoy the wildlife puppet theatre. They can learn about the fur trade while handling real beaver pelts or sit in the birch-bark winter wigwam and listen to a recorded story told by a Mi'kmaq elder. A canoe on springs allows kids to experience what it's like to paddle through whitewater, while also teaching water safety.

The Voyageur Encampment invites visitors to climb beneath an overturned 36-foot *canot du maitre* and imagine falling asleep along the banks of the French River. You can try your hand at the voyageur's life by lugging a 90-pound (40 kg) canoe pack or by attempting to paddle 50 to 60 strokes per minute, just as the voyageurs did.

The museum hosts one-of-a-kind paddling tours geared to people of all ages and abilities, so check their website for future events.

80 CROSS-COUNTRY SKIING IN MUSKOKA

~ Muskoka

Muskoka is a legendary summer paradise. Generations of well-heeled cottagers escape Ontario's sweltering hubs of commerce and race north to rusticate and recharge. Some even make the trip in autumn. By winter, they are gone, and Muskoka becomes an equally idyllic playground for those who enjoy cross-country skiing or snowshoeing.

LEFT: White-tailed deer are taken by surprise. BELOW: Muskoka's many trails make it an ideal destination for cross-country skiing and snowshoeing. FACING PAGE: A red fox steps gingerly through new snow in search of prey.

Things to See & Do

- Visit Arrowhead Provincial Park for some of the best cross-country skiing in Ontario.
- Enter the annual Muskoka Loppet.
- Ski the scenic trails along the Muskoka River.
- Watch for winter wildlife sightings.

Muskoka Tourism
1342 Highway 11 North
Kilworthy, ON P0E 1G0
1-800-267-9700
discovermuskoka.ca/
    things-to-do/
    cross-country-skiing

The region's many parks and resorts possess some of Ontario's best-groomed trails, at a wide range of distances, and host several major cross-country skiing events. Arrowhead Provincial Park, near Huntsville, was the site of the 2013 Canadian Masters Cross-Country Ski Championships.

Located seven kilometres (4.3 mi) north of Huntsville off Highway 11, Arrowhead Provincial Park maintains more than 33 kilometres (20.5 mi) of ski trails designed for classic cross-country skiing or skate-skiing. The trails are rated according to difficulty, from beginner to expert. The park also offers several hiking and snowshoeing trails, even an ice-skating trail. The Arrowhead Nordic Ski Club runs programs and events within Arrowhead Provincial Park, including the annual Muskoka Loppet race for all ages and levels, at five kilometres (3 mi), 10 kilometres (5 mi) and 15 kilometres (9 mi).

Also near Huntsville, the Limberlost Forest and Wildlife Reserve is a publicly accessible year-round wilderness haven with 20 lakes and some 4,050 hectares (10,000 acres) of mixed forest. This privately owned and operated forest reserve features more than 70 kilometres (44 mi) of hiking, biking, skiing and snowshoeing trails that are available to the public at no charge. The reserve maintains 25 kilometres (15.5 mi) of groomed trails throughout winter.

Bracebridge Resource Management Centre, along Highway 11, north of

Bracebridge, offers 16.5 kilometres (10 mi) of groomed trails for cross-country skiing. The wooded trails range from about one to eight kilometres (0.6–5 mi) in length and feature frequent scenic glimpses of the Muskoka River. There is no fee to use the trails.

The Gravenhurst/Muskoka KOA, at 1083 Reay Road (off Highway 11, south of Muskoka Airport), offers 15 kilometres (9 mi) of groomed and track-set cross-country ski trails spread over 358 hectares (885 acres) of wilderness.

Several resorts have their own groomed trails: the Bay-view Wildwood Resort in Gravenhurst has eight kilometres (5 mi); Cedar Grove Lodge and Deerhurst Resort in Huntsville have seven and five kilometres (4.3 and 3 mi), respectively; Bondi Village, Lake of Bays, has 15 kilometres (9 mi).

Cross-country skiing is a wonderful way to discover winter wildlife. Watch for ruffed grouse, wild turkeys, white-tailed deer, moose and pine martens. Muskoka's fox population thrives during the winter, so be on the lookout. There is little as startling as suddenly witnessing a fox leap out of the snow while in pursuit of a mouse or hare.

The region's many parks and resorts possess some of Ontario's best-groomed trails, at a wide variety of lengths.

81 FATHOM FIVE NATIONAL MARINE PARK & FLOWERPOT ISLAND

~ Tobermory

Snorkelling at Fathom Five National Marine Park: The park has the clearest deep water of any location in the Great Lakes.

Located at the tip of the Bruce Peninsula, Fathom Five National Marine Park offers the clearest deep water to be found among the Great Lakes, which makes it a top destination for paddlers and divers.

In fact, Fathom Five provides some of the world's best freshwater diving, with dramatic underwater cliffs, caves and overhangs, as well as 22 historic shipwrecks — something for divers at all skill levels and excellent for snorkellers. The Parks Canada website provides a map and a list of dive sites. Divers must register and purchase a diving pass from the park's Visitor Centre or from one of Tobermory's dive shops. No permit is required to snorkel.

In 1987, Fathom Five became Canada's first National Marine Conservation Area, the result of a dedicated campaign to protect and preserve its 20 islands, ancient rock formations, cliff-clinging forests, its many species of orchids and ferns and also to acknowledge the cultural legacy of its light stations and shipwrecks.

The rock rising up through these pristine waters is as much as 420 million years old. Perhaps the most striking geological formations in the park are the isolated flowerpot-shaped pillars (or sea stacks) found on Flowerpot Island. The strange flowerpots are the creation of thousands of years of erosion. Over time, wind, rain and waves have eaten away at the cliff face, leaving standing columns of softer sedimentary rock topped by harder protective caprock.

Things to See & Do

- Hike to the towering Flowerpots.
- Kayak the rugged shoreline.
- Snorkel or dive among the shipwrecks.
- Visit Big Tub lighthouse.

Visitor Centre
120 Chi sin tib dek Road
Tobermory, ON
N0H 2R0
519-596-2233
1-877-773-8888
pc.gc.ca/en/
amnc-nmca/on/
fathomfive

Flowerpot Island is 6.5 kilometres (4 mi) from Tobermory harbour and is accessible only by boat. Two private tour-boat companies offer return-trip service from mid-May to mid-October. Park staff recommend that only seasoned paddlers attempt the crossing by canoe or kayak.

The island is about 198 hectares (490 acres) in size. Most visitors start at Beachy Cove, on the southeastern shore, and hike north to the flowerpots, then on to the island's cave and light station — about a three-hour trip if you backtrack along the same trail. The first flowerpot tower, the lesser of the two, stands approximately seven metres (23 ft) tall. The second, taller flowerpot stands 12 metres (39 ft). A third flowerpot existed but toppled in 1903. Farther up the trail is the island's light station, maintained by the Friends of Bruce District Parks.

For a more adventurous hike, continue around the full loop trail, which leads through rocky terrain with steep stairs at two points. The loop option — past the flowerpots, cave, light station, with a return via the island's interior Mountain Trail — takes about four to five hours and is a satisfying way to spend a day.

BELOW: The ghostly image of a sunken ship at Fathom Five Park. The park's 22 shipwrecks attract divers from all over the world. FOLLOWING PAGES: The ancient sea stack formations that give Flowerpot Island its name.

82

FRENCH RIVER PROVINCIAL PARK

~ Alban

Things to See & Do

- See the "Voices of the River" exhibit in the architecturally cool Visitor Centre.
- Paddle the route of Indigenous travellers, French and English explorers and fur traders.
- Choose from more than 50 lodges along the river.
- Kayak the beautiful French River Delta.

Visitor Centre
20526 Highway 69
P.O. Box 9
Alban, ON P0M 1A0
705-857-1630 summer
705-287-2900 winter
ontarioparks.com/park/
frenchriver

The French River has been a major transportation route for Indigenous peoples for thousands of years, as evidenced by the waterway's many pictographs and archaeological sites. Research suggests that Shield Archaic and Algonquian peoples used the route, followed by the Huron and Ojibwe, who called the river *Wemitigoj-Sibi* ("French River") as it came to be associated with 17th-century French explorers and missionaries.

Étienne Brulé first paddled its waters in 1604, and Samuel de Champlain arrived soon after him. Explorers Jean Nicollet, Pierre Radisson, des Groseillers and La Verendrye travelled the river between 1629 and 1649; still later, Simon Fraser, Alexander Mackenzie and David Thompson. Together with the Ottawa and Mattawa rivers, the French River became part of the fur-trade water route linking Montreal and Lake Superior.

The upper portion of the French River flows through the rugged glaciated granite and heavily forested areas typical of the Canadian Shield. At the mouth of the river, countless islands are defined by an equal number of channels. These form narrow, steep-walled gorges, foaming falls and rapids, which eventually lead to broad expanses of open water. (Georgian Bay coastal kayaking is available via the French River Delta.) But because of the rugged topography surrounding the French River, large parts of it remain relatively untouched.

In honour of its significance in the history of Canada, in 1986, the French River became the first designated Canadian Heritage River. In 1989, in an attempt to protect its wilderness in perpetuity, the river was made part of the Ontario Provincial Parks system.

French River Provincial Park totals 73,530 hectares (181,697 acres). The river flows 110 kilometres (68 mi) through interconnected lakes, gorges and rapids, from Lake Nipissing to Georgian Bay.

Paddlers can choose from multiple routes along the river, including inter-

LEFT: The award-winning French River Visitor Centre on Highway 69 was designed in partnership with local Métis and First Nations. FACING PAGE: Canoeing past Pine Cove on the French River.

The upper portion of the French River flows through rugged glaciated granite and heavily forested areas typical of the Canadian Shield.

connecting routes with the Restoule and Little French rivers. The river is navigable both upstream and downstream under non-flood conditions, but during spring runoff, it can rise as much as four metres (13 ft) at some points. At Recollet Falls, in the French River Gorge, there is no option for passable portage during spring runoff.

There are 13 access points along the river. The majority of these are occupied by outfitters and tourism operations, which issue park permits on behalf of Ontario Parks. French River interior camping permits are also available at Restoule Provincial Park for those entering via the Restoule River. There are 230 undeveloped backcountry campsites along the river. The campsites are marked and are available on a first-come, first-served basis.

As fishing is a very popular activity on the French, there are more than 50 lodges and marinas along its shores. Walleye, smallmouth bass, northern pike and muskellunge top the list of fishable species.

The award-winning French River Visitor Centre on Highway 69 was designed by Baird Sampson Neuert Architects, in partnership with local Métis and First Nations. The Centre's "Voices of the River" exhibit showcases the rich history of Indigenous, French and English cultures that have travelled these waters over the centuries.

83

HALIBURTON SCULPTURE FOREST

～ Haliburton

The Haliburton Sculpture Forest, in Glebe Park near the village of Haliburton, is a unique collection of outdoor sculptures created by Canadian and international artists. The trails here — suitable for walking and bike riding in spring, summer and fall and cross-country skiing and snowshoeing in the winter — provide changing perspectives of the forest and the sculptures in each of the seasons, so every visit seems fresh.

The Haliburton Sculpture Forest began as a project of the Arts Committee of the Haliburton County Development Corporation, with a goal to foster local economic development through the arts and create an outdoor visual arts destination in Haliburton County that would attract both residents and visitors year-round. The official opening of the Sculpture Forest took place in autumn of 2001 with the installation of three sculptures.

RIGHT: *Together We Explore the Wild Forest*, salt and pepper granite, by George Pratt. FACING PAGE, CLOCKWISE FROM TOP LEFT: *Sleep of the Huntress*, Belmont rose granite, by Doug Stephens; *Spiral Ascent*, locally quarried granite, by John Rimmington-Shaw and 2015 Dry Stone Structures students; *Redwing Frond*, steel and acrylic panels, by Darlene Bolahood; *A Conspiracy of Ravens*, with fans, bronze and steel, by John McKinnon.

In 2004, a new campus for Fleming College's Haliburton School of Art + Design was built in Glebe Park, with the Sculpture Forest trail surrounding the college and serving as a teaching site for many of its programs. Over the years, this fascinating forest gallery has grown by more than tenfold, with sculptures that boldly assert themselves and those that nestle more naturally among the trees.

The sculptures run the gamut from representational to abstract art and are variously formed from granite, limestone, springstone, polished concrete, steel, iron, bronze, wire, glass, acrylic, wood, old farm implements and found metal objects. Some are ethereal, others whimsical. Some relate to the Haliburton landscape, others to its history.

Today, the Sculpture Forest is an ongoing initiative of Haliburton Sculpture Forest et al., a not-for-profit organization whose purpose is "to increase understanding and appreciation of the arts through the development of public art and the engagement of artists with the community."

The Sculpture Forest is ideal for families looking for an interesting (even educational) outing, as well as for individuals in search of an inspiring walk and a rare artistic experience. The listed website offers a map of the Sculpture Forest and information about the artists and their work. A site map is available at the entrance to the forest, and while admission is free, contributions to the donation box are welcome.

A free guided tour of the Sculpture Forest is offered at 10 o'clock each Tuesday morning in July and August. On Wednesday mornings at 12:10, visitors are invited to join in a 40-minute "Curator's Selection Tour."

The Sculpture Forest shares the park with the Haliburton Highlands Museum and the Haliburton Campus of Fleming College, home to the Haliburton School of Art + Design — great places to visit after you tour the Sculpture Forest.

Things to See & Do

- Visit the Sculpture Forest in all seasons.
- Take the trail with a friend and compare favourite sculptures.
- Read about each work and its artist(s) online.
- Pay a visit to Haliburton Highlands Museum and Haliburton School of Art + Design.

Haliburton Sculpture Forest
297 College Drive
Haliburton, ON
K0M 1S0
705-457-3555
haliburtonsculpture
 forest.ca

84 ICE FISHING ON LAKE SIMCOE

~ Lake Simcoe

Lake Simcoe-area residents call their lake the Ice Fishing Capital of the World. Of course, so do a few other communities. But on a sunny winter day when the fish are biting and the wind isn't, it seems like a reasonable claim.

On a good, cold winter weekend, there may be as many as 6,000 anglers on Lake Simcoe's ice surface. While that sounds like a big chunk of humanity, it's worth noting that Simcoe is a big lake. Covering 743 square kilometres (287 sq mi) and fairly shallow, it is a perfect lake for ice fishing.

The Canadian Ice Fishing Championships (CIFC) are held on the lake in late February, with over $50,000 in prizes. Additional trophies are presented for the Biggest Whitefish, Biggest Lake Trout, Top Scoring Male, Top Scoring Female and Top Scoring Mixed Doubles Couple. Eight professionally trained officials score fish and make sure everyone follows CIFC rules.

The potential catch is diverse, with perch, walleye, pike, trout, herring, whitefish, bass and even muskellunge. The warmer winters experienced in recent years have restricted fishing to the shallow waters close to shore, where perch abound, but a colder winter yields plenty of lake trout, walleye and whitefish. Bait choice depends on what you're after. Many ice fishermen jig with grubs, cut bait, cheese balls or solid lures, but others swear by a jigging lure called the Swed-

BELOW: John Whyte with lake trout.
BELOW RIGHT: Yvonne Brown, from Ontario Women Anglers, with Dave Chong, Big Jim McLaughlin and Wil Wegman. This group of ice-fishing experts travels across the province every winter to present ice-fishing seminars.

Despite being Ontario's most intensely ice-fished inland body of water, Lake Simcoe still offers up places where it's possible to access the vast lake and find no other anglers.

Things to See & Do

- Rent a hut near near your preferred spot.
- Visit your fishing outfitter for the latest gear.
- Take your properly attired friends and/or loved ones.
- Enter a tournament or just enjoy being Canadian.

Tourism Simcoe County
1151 Highway 26
West Minesing, ON
L9X 0Z7
1-800-487-6642
experience.simcoe.ca

ish Pimple, described as one of the 50 greatest lures of all time by *Field and Stream*.

Ice and sun make a beautiful combination, but be sure to consult local outfitters regarding ice thickness and safety. Pressure ridges can build up in various spots on a lake, and some areas may be thinner than others. Hut operators routinely scout the ice, check its thickness and establish safe travel routes for foot traffic, snowmobiles, ATVs and full-sized vehicles.

Holes are generally made with powered augers or large chainsaws. When you rent a hut, the guy from the rental company is usually happy to cut a hole for you when he delivers the hut. There are more than 30 hut rental agencies in the Lake Simcoe region. Portable huts may be rented by the day or by the week. Some outfitters offer full ice-fishing vacations, with a heated fishing hut, a pre-cut hole, a regularly replenished supply of bait, transportation to and from your hut, meal deliveries and several nights in a local bed-and-breakfast.

By law (and common sense), all ice huts have to be removed from the ice on Lake Simcoe by March 15.

85 KILLARNEY PROVINCIAL PARK & THE LA CLOCHE MOUNTAINS

～ Killarney

Killarney Provincial Park offers 183 backcountry canoe-in camping sites.

The La Cloche Mountains that run through Killarney Provincial Park are an estimated 3.5 billion years old. They are one of the oldest mountain ranges on Earth and once stood taller than the present-day Rocky Mountains. Today, though striking, they appear more like massive, rounded stone hills. Over the past million years or so, four ice ages have scraped away the mountaintops, leaving the distinct white quartzite ridges that now dominate the landscape and reflect in the park's clear cerulean waters.

Although they may lack their former high-peaked glory, the La Cloche Mountains' distinctive appearance has attracted artists and writers, canoeists and hikers for well over a century. In fact, it was due to a lobby by artists, including founding Group of Seven member A. Y. Jackson, that the Ontario government made Killarney a provincial park.

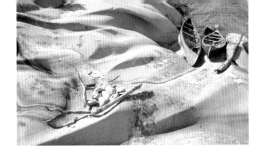

LEFT: Canoes moored on wave-smoothed stone in Killarney Provincial Park. BELOW: Worn down by four ice ages, the La Cloche Mountains once rose higher than the Rockies.

Things to See & Do

- Climb some of the oldest rock on Earth.
- View the vista from atop Killarney Ridge.
- Paddle the park's pristine waterways.
- Photograph the abundant wildlife.

General Information
960 Highway 637
Killarney, ON P0M 2A0
705-287-2900
1-888-668-7275
ontarioparks.com/park/
killarney

The park lies in the transition zone between northern boreal forest and the St. Lawrence–Great Lakes lowlands, providing habitat for an unusually diverse range of plants and animals. Mammals include typical northern species such as moose, deer, wolves, bobcat, marten and beaver, but more than 20 species of reptiles and amphibians can also be found in the park.

Killarney offers 183 backcountry canoe-in sites and 33 backcountry hike-in sites. There is also car camping available at George Lake Campground, as well as a couple of camp cabins and six yurts.

The five day-use trails range from one to four hours and from moderate to difficult. At six kilometres (3.7 mi), "The Crack" is the longest day-use trail. Strictly for seasoned hikers, it leads to a stunning view from the top of Killarney Ridge. If you have a few days to spend in the park, the La Cloche Silhouette Trail is a magnificent but challenging 80-kilometre (50 mi) loop that takes seven to 10 days to complete.

Much of the park is accessible year-round, and it is a popular destination for cross-country skiers and snowshoers in the winter.

86

MANITOULIN ISLAND INDIGENOUS ADVENTURES
∼ Manitoulin Island

BELOW: Sunset on the water at Providence Bay, Manitoulin Island. FACING PAGE, LEFT: A tipi decorated with traditional imagery. FACING PAGE, RIGHT: Swimmers at Bridal Veil Falls, near Kagawong.

Who better to show you the highlights of Lake Huron's vast Manitoulin Island and explain its Indigenous past than guides whose ancestors have inhabited this land for hundreds of years?

Through Wikwemikong Tourism, Manitoulin's largest First Nation community and Canada's only officially recognized Unceded Indian Reserve, offers a number of tours hosted by resident Anishnaabek guides. The Anishnaabek of the Three Fires Confederacy — Ojibwe, Odawa and Pottawatomi — share their history and legends and introduce visitors to Manitoulin's remarkable landscape.

The four-hour interpretive hike along the Bebamikawe Memorial Trail passes replica lodges and hunting shelters, in diverse habitat, before leading to stunning

Things to See & Do

- Hike the Bebamikawe Memorial Trail.
- Participate in a Dewegan drum-and-song session.
- Learn about the island's medicinal, edible and spiritual plants.
- Discover the importance of Indigenous cultures.

Wikwemikong Tourism
19 A Complex Drive
Wikwemikong, ON
P0P 2J0
705-859-3122
1-800-880-1406
wikwemikong.ca

Great Spirit Circle Trail
P.O. Box 469
5905 Highway 540
M'Chigeeng, ON
P0P 1G0
705-377-4404
1-877-710-3211
circletrail.com

views along the Niagara Escarpment. The three-hour Unceded Journey Tour takes you to four historic sites that tell the history of Manitoulin Island, including the treaties of 1836 and 1862, the now infamous "Manitoulin Incident," and the legend of Zhibzhii, the underwater spirit.

There are also options for historic canoe tours, overnight stays in an authentic Anishnaabek (Odawa) lodge, Dewegan drum and song experiences, educational hikes focused on edible and medicinal plants, wild bird and mammal identification hikes and painting sessions based on the teachings of the Seven Grandfathers.

The Wikwemikong Cultural Festival, held every Civic Holiday Weekend, features traditional dancers, drummers and singers from across North America.

Great Spirit Circle Trail also offers nature- and cultural-based tourism from an Aboriginal perspective. There are medicine walks, canoe heritage tours through the heart of the island, a Mother Earth hiking trail to the top of an 85-metre (280 ft) bluff and a Legends of the Land horseback-riding trip — all with qualified, knowledgeable Anishnaabek guides.

Those looking for less strenuous activities may choose the walking tour of art galleries, heritage museums and gift shops or perhaps a specialty workshop that teaches lodge building, teepee setup, traditional torch making, drum making, storytelling or traditional medicine harvesting.

MARIPOSA FOLK FESTIVAL
⤳ Orillia

The Mariposa Folk Festival is one of the longest-running folk festivals in North America. Like the music it promotes and preserves, the festival has weathered a lot of storms and proven itself a worthy survivor.

The festival began in Orillia in 1961, at the peak of the folk music revival. The first two festivals were peaceful events, but 1963 saw larger, rowdier crowds that alarmed the town council. The 1964 lineup featured Buffy Saint-Marie and Gordon Lightfoot — playing at an aging baseball diamond in Toronto. From 1967 to 1979, the festival found a home on Toronto Island. The 1980s brought a Molson

RIGHT: Bruce Cockburn performs a seated acoustic set at the Mariposa Folk Festival. FACING PAGE, LEFT TO RIGHT: Children drum and sing in the interactive Folkplay area; Whitehorse (Luke Doucet and Melissa McClelland) give an enthusiastic nighttime performance; Edmonton singer-songwriter Ruth B engages the crowd.

Breweries sponsorship and a move to Barrie. The 1990s saw more relocations and a lot of rain, but organizers remained committed.

Thus far, Mariposa stages had presented a who's who of folk-roots performers, among them Pete Seeger, Joni Mitchell, Joan Baez, Doc Watson, Leonard Cohen, Richie Havens, Murray McLaughlin, Cat Stevens, Bob Dylan, Neil Young, John Prine, Bruce Cockburn, the McGarrigle Sisters, Taj Mahal, Stan Rogers, Leon Redbone, Jackson Browne, Emmylou Harris, John Hiatt, Loreena McKennitt, Arlo Guthrie, Melissa Etheridge, Guy Clark, Roger McGuinn and Donovan.

Finally, in 2000, with renewed local support, the Mariposa Folk Festival was brought back home to Orillia, where it has remained ever since. And for more years than not, the sun has shone with approval.

Today, the three-day Mariposa Festival includes music, spoken word and dance, with over 100 performances on 11 stages in J. B. Tudhope Memorial Park. Organizers invite audience members of all ages to participate in folk culture. There are dozens of interactive workshops — songwriting, hand drumming, dancing, painting, craft making — as well as yoga and tai chi sessions in the park. The Folkplay area is a safe, creative place for children, with interactive concerts on the Sunshine Stage and the opportunity to experiment with musical instruments, dance, fly kites, make bubbles and just have fun.

Food vendors are selected for value, quality and range of choices, offering everything from barbecue to vegetarian fare to ethnic cuisine. Beer, cider, wine and coolers can be found at Mariposa's Pub Tent.

The popular Artisans' Village showcases the work of 50 artisans, designers and craftspeople whose unique handcrafted works, including musical instruments, carvings, weaving, clothing, paintings, pottery, glasswork, jewellery, and more, are available for purchase.

Tudhope Park juts out into the waters of Lake Couchiching, and supervised Moose Beach is a great place to swim and cool off, so bring your bathing suit.

Things to See & Do

- Hear the best of traditional and new folk-roots music.
- Participate in a songwriting workshop.
- View the well-crafted wares in the Artisans' Village.
- Be a part of Mariposa Folk Festival history.

Mariposa Folk Festival
10 Peter Street South
Orillia, ON L3V 5A9
705-326-3655
mariposafolk.com

88 "MINERAL CAPITAL OF CANADA"

～ Bancroft

Nearly 90 percent of all the types of minerals on Earth can be found in the Bancroft and North Hastings area. Perhaps rightly, Bancroft lays claim to the title "Mineral Capital of Canada," and collectors turn out by the hundreds for its annual Rockhound Gemboree, Canada's largest gem and mineral show.

This part of the Canadian Shield was formed approximately 1.35 billion years ago, and much of the topography from Bancroft south to Madoc is dominated by intrusive igneous rock (plutonic rock) that crystallized as magma slowly cooled below the Earth's surface. This process — with its variations in pressure and temperature — was ideal for the formation of the gemstone tourmaline and crystals of similar origin. Venting produced quartz veins, some of which contain gold and silver.

The Bancroft Gem and Mineral Club Mineral Museum provides a good orientation, with over 400 mineral specimens from the surrounding area. Exhibits cover much of the region's mining history, though there is little active mining going on today.

A popular spot for visitors is the Eagle's Nest lookout, just north of the town. This 60-metre (197 ft) cliff overlooks the densely wooded York River Valley and the town of Bancroft. Another popular location is a series of abandoned mineral caves and mines at Egan's Chute, northeast of Bancroft on Highway 28.

You don't have to be a mineral expert to enjoy Bancroft. Visitors can pan for gold, learn about mineral identification from the museum's geologists and take part in guided mineral-collecting field trips. Field-trip participants must wear closed footwear and supply their own safety glasses and basic rockhounding equipment, such as a rock hammer, shovel, chisel, bucket, etc.

Of course, there's a quicker route to finding those sought-after stones. The Princess Sodalite Mine Rock Shop on Highway 28 sells all manner of rocks, minerals, gemstones, healing crystals, jewellery and rock crafts and more. The ever-changing selection ranges from beginner quality to museum grade. The shop also carries an expanding selection of fossil specimens. Its namesake mine continues to produce sodalite, from collector specimens to large display pieces.

Held each August, the Rockhound Gemboree has been going strong for over 45 years. The event brings together more than 100 dealers of fine mineral specimens, gemstones, jewellery and lapidary (engraving, cutting, polishing) supplies.

Traditionally held at the Bancroft Curling Club and North Hastings Community Centre, with a shuttle service between the two venues, the Gemboree features keynote speakers, demonstrations, workshops, swapper tents and exhibits of rocks, crystals, gems, fossils and one-of-a-kind jewellery and art pieces. ～

Things to See & Do

- Learn about the area's hidden treasures at the Bancroft Gem and Mineral Club Mineral Museum.
- View the "Mineral Capital" view from the Eagle's Nest lookout.
- Take part in a guided mineral-collecting field trip.
- Attend the famous Rockhound Gemboree.

Town of Bancroft
8 Hastings Heritage Way
P.O. Box 790
Bancroft, ON K0L 1C0
613-332-333

ABOVE: An early-morning view of the town of Bancroft from the Eagle's Nest lookout. LEFT: A sodalite sample, with its distinctive bluish hue. In 1906, 130 tons of local sodalite were shipped across the Atlantic to decorate the Princess of Wales' royal residence.

89

MOOSE SAFARIS & WOLF HOWLS
∼ Algonquin Provincial Park

Paddle quietly down its rivers and along Algonquin Provincial Park lakeshores, and you are sure to see moose, deer, beaver and other of the more than 50 species of woodland mammals that call the park home. Algonquin boasts some 30 reptile and amphibian species, 54 fish species, more than 130 species of breeding birds, and (worth noting) about 7,000 insect species. Bring insect repellent in spring and summer.

Algonquin has the distinction of being Ontario's first provincial park, established in 1893. It occupies 7,630 square kilometres (2,946 sq mi)) of land and water, so there is abundant room for all these species and about a half million annual visitors (most of whom stick to the outskirts of the park).

One of the park's greatest attractions is wildlife viewing. There are whitetailed deer, great gray owls, beavers, otters and red foxes. While there are rare glimpses of black bears and wolves, the trophy sightings, hands down, are moose.

Things to See & Do

- Keep a log of the many creatures you encounter.
- Canoe for days.
- Learn about park wildlife from the Friends of Algonquin.
- Participate in a Wolf Howl.

General Information
Highway 60, P.O. Box 219
Whitney, ON K0J 2M0
705-633-5572
ontarioparks.com/park/
  algonquin
algonquinpark.on.ca
  (The Friends of
  Algonquin Park)

Algonquin Park offers your best chance in the province to see a moose.

The easiest route to a sighting is to drive Highway 60 in springtime, when moose are attracted to the roadsides by the salt left over from winter road maintenance. But it's far more rewarding to explore the park's bogs, ponds and beaver meadows early in the day. Open areas near the cover of thick forest are excellent places to spot wildlife. Several regional outfitters offer "moose safaris" and wildlife photography expeditions. (Warning: If a moose flattens its ears against its body, give it a bit more space.)

Many people avoid wilderness camping for fear of bears. Although there are an estimated 2,000 black bears in Algonquin Park, it is highly unlikely that you will encounter one. Most bears are shy of humans unless they've had luck finding food at campsites. Please learn and follow proper camping protocol.

Supervised wolf howl expeditions are held on Thursdays in August or in September before Labour Day, weather permitting and dependent on wolf proximity. Amateur naturalists of all ages gather at the park's Outdoor Theatre for a presentation on wolf ecology before setting out to attempt call-and-response sessions with any wolf packs near by. The Howl is popular and has been added to the Winter in the Wild event, held Family Day Weekend in February.

90

MUSKOKA STEAMSHIPS & DISCOVERY CENTRE

~ Gravenhurst

The *Wenonah* first steamed across Lake Muskoka in 1866, a year before Canada became a nation. The *Wenonah II* steams the lakes today, a modern interpretation of that early traditional steamship.

Her mate, the RMS (Royal Mail Ship) *Segwun* was built in Glasgow, Scotland, in 1887 and assembled in Gravenhurst. The ship was originally a side-paddlewheel steamer named *Nipissing II* and transported passengers, mail and freight from Muskoka Wharf in Gravenhurst to the cottages and resorts that were springing up on the Muskoka Lakes shorelines. Alas, the *Nipissing II* was withdrawn from service by 1914, but 10 years later, in 1924, her superstructure was rebuilt and twin-propeller engines were ordered from Scotland. In 1925, the ship launched anew, with a new Ojibwe name, *Segwun*, meaning "Springtime."

The new steamer proved to be the fastest ship on the lakes and continued her service to Canada Post until 1958. With improved roads and mail delivery taking place over land routes, the *Segwun* made her last trip before being decommissioned. In 1962, she escaped deconstruction when she was converted into a floating maritime museum at Gravenhurst Wharf.

With the help of steamship enthusiasts from the Muskoka Steamship & Historical Society and the Ontario Road Builders, the *Segwun* was relaunched in 1974. In 1981, further restoration led to a new career as a cruise ship on the Muskoka Lakes. Each summer, thousands of tourists experience the beauty of Muskoka aboard the *Segwun*, North America's oldest operating hand-fired steamship. The *Segwun* requires more than 250 tons of coal to fuel her four-and-a-half-month transportation season on Muskoka waters. The ship can also be chartered for corporate and private events.

Built in 2002, in the style of a 1907 Muskoka vessel, *Wenonah II* also offers cruises on all three Muskoka Lakes. Passengers enjoy three upscale dining rooms and three decks.

The Muskoka Discovery Centre is home to Mrs. Timothy Eaton's 1915 *Wanda III*, once equipped to cruise the lakes at an unparalleled 24 miles per hour. Other gems reside in the Murray Walker Grace and Speed Boathouse, which houses North America's largest collection of in-water classic antique wooden boats. The collection is ever-changing as the boats are privately owned and on display through the generosity of their owners.

The Discovery Centre's museum looks at the history of the region's Indigenous people and early settlers and the use of various wooden watercraft and steamships, with interactive exhibits for all ages. ~

Things to See & Do

- Take a cruise aboard the RMS *Segwun*.
- Admire the antique boats in the Murray Walker Grace and Speed Boathouse.
- Check out Mrs. Timothy Eaton's *Wanda III*.
- See some of the oldest maps of the Muskoka Lakes.

Muskoka Steamships & Discovery Centre
185 Cherokee Lane
Gravenhurst, ON
P1P 1Z9
705-687-6667
1-866-687-6667
realmuskoka.com

CLOCKWISE FROM BELOW LEFT: The SS *Sagamo* once ferried passengers from Muskoka Wharf in Gravenhurst to Beaumaris, Port Carling, Windermere and the Royal Muskoka Hotel; the Muskoka Discovery Centre houses North America's largest collection of in-water antique wooden boats; the *Segwun* is North America's oldest operating hand-fired steamship.

91

PADDLEPALOOZA KAYAK FESTIVAL

~ Parry Sound

Ontario's wealth of large lakes and wide rivers means that, no matter where you live in the province, great sea kayaking is never more than a short drive away. That said, Georgian Bay is considered a mecca for sea kayakers. Each May, the Ontario Sea Kayak Centre hosts its tune-up Paddlepalooza Kayak Festival in Parry Sound. The Sound's sheltered inlets and access to the open waters of Georgian Bay make it an ideal location.

Based in Parry Sound, the Ontario Sea Kayak Centre (OSKC) has become one of Canada's leading sea-kayaking schools, and its Paddlepalooza is now the largest annual sea-kayaking event in Ontario. The combination of perfect water and ease of accessibility from southern cities has attracted top-tier professional coaches and paddlers at every skill level.

Recent Paddlepaloozas have used the YWCA's Camp Tapawingo, south of Parry Sound, at the Two Mile Narrows, for meals and accommodation. This location enables paddlers to launch from the camp's beach and practise in sheltered waters before paddling toward Five Mile Bay, shuttling farther south to Moon River to work on moving-water techniques or heading for the open waters of Georgian Bay for classes in open-water rescues, surf skills and navigation.

Visiting instructors from other paddling schools in Ontario, Quebec and the United States augment the OSKC teaching staff for this weekend event. Sample courses and seminars might include such topics as Kayak Fundamentals & Tour of the Sound, Refining Your Roll, Moving Water Moves, Fundamental Strokes Tune-up, Maneuvering with Blended Strokes, Powerful Forward Paddling, Traditional Greenland-style Kayaking, Technical and Tactical Touring Skills, Sculling for Support, Navigation and Weather for the Great Lakes and the Seas, Speedy Self-Rescue Tips and Tricks, What to Do When Stuff Goes Wrong, and Tarpology and Kayak Trip Packing.

Outside of class time, there's a gear-swap garage sale, a Greenland paddle carving demonstration, rolling playtime at the waterfront, drop-in yoga, live music on Saturday night and the Reel Paddling Film Festival.

In addition to Paddlepalooza, the OSKC hosts North America's largest women-only paddling event, the Women on the Water Festival, in June; conducts summer courses in multiple Ontario locations; offers guided sea-kayaking adventures throughout Ontario, Canada and internationally; and in September operates its Ontario Greenland Camp, Canada's longest-running traditional paddling event.

For those seeking something slightly less rustic and rigorous, the Ontario Sea

Things to See & Do

- Take courses from top-notch sea-kayaking instructors.
- Refine your roll and your moving-water moves.
- Learn to carve a Greenland-style paddle.
- Attend the Reel Paddling Film Festival.

Ontario Sea Kayaking Centre
6 Harmony Lane
Parry Sound, ON
P2A 0B1
905-399-1216
ontarioseakayakcentre. com

Kayak Centre recommends its sister company, Parry Sound's Harmony Outdoor Inn, which offers both glamping (luxury camping) and high-end bed-and-breakfast service. The Inn is located on a wooded 6.5-hectare (16 acres) waterfront location, with options for paddling courses, private skills-development sessions and Georgian Bay day trips.

Based in Parry Sound, the Ontario Sea Kayak Centre (OSKC) has become one of Canada's leading sea-kayaking schools, and its Paddlepalooza is now the largest annual sea-kayaking event in Ontario.

92

PETROGLYPHS PROVINCIAL PARK & NATIONAL HISTORIC SITE

~ Woodview/Peterborough

Petroglyphs Provincial Park, a cultural heritage-class park located near Woodview, northeast of Peterborough, contains the largest known concentration of Aboriginal rock carvings (petroglyphs) in Canada.

Known as *Kinomagewapkong*, or "the Teaching Rocks," by the area's Ojibwe, the carvings depict symbolic shapes, human figures (perhaps shamans), birds, mammals, reptiles, fish, supernatural creatures and a dominant figure with a sunlike head, which may represent the Great Spirit.

The approximately 1,200 images were carved five to eight centimetres (2–3 in)

RIGHT: The Learning Place Visitor Centre is operated by members of the Curve Lake First Nation and features displays about the petroglyphs and their significance to First Nations people. FACING PAGE, LEFT AND RIGHT: There are four parks trails: Ratarat Trail, Marsh Trail, Nanabush Trail and West Day-Use Trail, all rated easy to moderate; at the Visitor Centre, a film entitled *The Teaching Rocks* is shown daily, and there is a hands-on activity area for children.

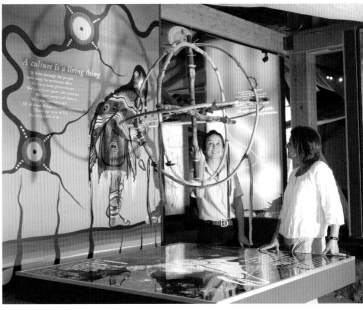

Things to See & Do

- Visit the 1,200 ancient Aboriginal petroglyphs.
- Try to decipher the images and stories.
- Visit the Learning Place Visitor Centre to learn more.
- Hike to beautiful, meromictic McGinnis Lake.

Learning Place
Visitor Centre
2249 Northey's Bay Road
Woodview, ON
K0L 3E0
705-877-2552
ontarioparks.com/park/petroglyphs

deep into this broad outcrop of white marble, probably by Algonquian- or Iroquian-speaking people, sometime between 900 and 1100 AD. Considered a monument to the artistic ability and spirituality of the early Aboriginal carvers, the petroglyphs have been designated a National Historic Site of Canada.

The petroglyphs came to public attention in 1954 when a prospector named Everett Davis accidently stumbled upon the location. They were first thoroughly recorded in 1965 and 1968 by Joan Vastokas of the University of Toronto and Romas Vastokas of Trent University in Peterborough. They have fascinated petroglyph scholars ever since.

According to the Learning Place Visitor Centre, the entire rock site is a sacred place and remains a place of pilgrimage for the region's Ojibwe people. Deep crevices in the rock are thought to lead to the spirit world, and the trickle of water that runs beneath the rock produces sounds that have been interpreted as those of the Spirits.

The Learning Place Visitor Centre is operated by members of the Curve Lake First Nation and features displays about the petroglyphs and their spiritual significance to First Nations people. A film entitled *The Teaching Rocks* is shown daily, and there is a hands-on activity area for children.

The petroglyphs occupy a relatively small area of the park, which is 1,643-hectare (4,060 acres). The rest is primarily woodland habitat, with opportunities for wildlife watching, including the provincially rare five-lined skink.

There are four parks trails: Ratarat Trail, Marsh Trail, Nanabush Trail and West Day-Use Trail, all rated easy to moderate. The shortest, Ratarat, leads to bright aquamarine McGinnis Lake, one of the few meromictic (water layers that don't intermix) lakes in Canada. In order to preserve the lake's unique meromictic state, swimming is prohibited.

93

SAINTE-MARIE AMONG THE HURONS NATIONAL HISTORIC SITE

~ Midland

BELOW and FACING PAGE, BOTTOM: A reconstructed 17th-century church and Jesuit residence at Sainte-Marie Among the Hurons. FACING PAGE, TOP: Carefully tended gardens provided essential food for the community.

Sainte-Marie Among the Hurons was a French Jesuit settlement in Wendake, the land of the Wendat, near modern Midland, Ontario, from 1639 to 1649. It was the first European settlement in what is now the province of Ontario. The reconstructed settlement allows visitors to imagine the world as it existed on these lands more than 370 years ago.

Open daily from May to October, this living museum takes visitors back to a time of first cross-cultural contact. A colourful audio-visual presentation sets the stage for the rest of your tour. Historic site maps and audio wands provide tour information in English, French, German, Italian, Spanish, Portuguese, Japanese, Dutch, Polish, Russian, Cantonese and Mandarin.

The mission was established in 1639 by 18 men, among them Fathers Jérôme Lalemant and Jean de Brébeuf. Structures were built near the Huron settlement of Quieunonascaranas — a chapel, a residence for the Jesuit brothers, a cookhouse and a blacksmith shop, among other buildings. Sainte-Marie became the Jesuit base for their ministry among the Iroquouian-speaking Huron and Petun, and the Algonquian-speaking Nipissing, Ottawa and Ojibwe.

The next 10 years involved high drama — the arrival of an unwanted French military presence, a smallpox epidemic, conflict between the Indigenous peoples who converted to Christianity and those who maintained their traditional beliefs, the Iroquois' purchase of firearms from Dutch traders, and war. On June 16, 1649, the missionaries chose to burn the mission rather than risk it being desecrated or permanently overrun by the Iroquois. Before the burning, the survivors decided that Brébeuf and Lalemant, who had been killed during the wars, would be canonized as martyrs. Ultimately, eight missionaries from Sainte-Marie were martyred.

Today, over the course of the summer, staff in historic costumes demonstrate 17th-century customs of European missionaries and Indigenous cultures. As you explore Sainte-Marie, you get a real sense of the challenges faced by the Jesuits and others who worked at this famous mission. Informative demonstrations and hands-on activities include 17th-century fire starting, clothing construction, cooking, early medicine and Indigenous games. Writing with quill pens is especially popular with iPad-age children.

Things to See & Do

- Imagine first contact between European missionaries and Indigenous people.
- Explore the reconstructed settlement in its 1639 condition.
- Learn about 17th-century medicine.
- Try writing with a quill.

Sainte-Marie Among the Hurons
16164 Highway 12 East
Midland, ON L4R 4K8
705-526-7838
saintemarieamong
  thehurons.on.ca/sm/
  en/home

94
TRENT–SEVERN WATERWAY & PETERBOROUGH LIFT LOCK NATIONAL HISTORIC SITE

~ Trenton–Peterborough–Port Severn

The Trent–Severn Waterway connects of 386 kilometres (240 mi) of navigable lakes and rivers through central Ontario, joining Lake Ontario at Trenton to Lake Huron at Port Severn. Its major natural arteries include the Trent River, the Otonabee River, the Kawartha Lakes, Lake Simcoe, Lake Couchiching and the Severn River.

The canal was first surveyed as a logging route, and the first lock, which was built in 1833, opened a large area to navigation by steamship. Construction of three additional locks had commenced when the Upper Canada Rebellion of 1837 broke out. It was not until the 1880s that the waterway's expansion was revisited, with John A. Macdonald's government adding new locks and extending the route westward. And it was almost the turn of the century before pressure on Wilfrid Laurier's Liberals led to significant advancement. The canal reached both Peterborough and Lake Simcoe in 1904, but the completion of final sections were delayed by the First World War. The link to Trenton opened in 1918, followed by the link to Georgian Bay in early 1920, and the first complete passage through the waterway was made in July of that year.

RIGHT: Early morning at the Kirkfield Lift Lock on the Trent–Severn waterway. FACING PAGE: A fall photograph of the Peterborough Lift Lock, the highest hydraulic lift lock in the world.

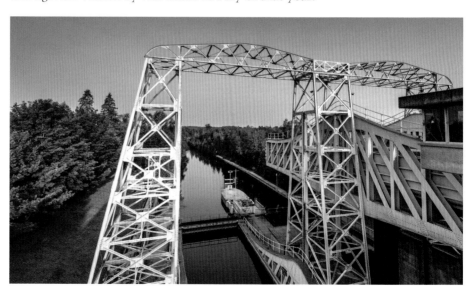

Alas, by the time of its completion, the Trent–Severn's potential as a commercial waterway was historical. Great Lakes ships were now larger than the canal could accommodate, and railways were handling much of the nation's freight.

The rise of pleasure boating saved the Trent–Severn from engineering oblivion. The waterway enabled boaters to travel leisurely through cottage country and beyond and made it a recreational cruising route that attracts thousands of visitors each year. Despite never having served its original purpose, this historic waterway has been called "one of the finest interconnected systems of navigation in the world."

The Trent–Severn has 45 locks, including 36 conventional locks, two sets of flight locks, hydraulic lift locks at Peterborough and Kirkfield and a marine railway at Big Chute that transports boats between the upper and lower sections of the Severn. The system also includes 39 swing bridges and 160 dams and other control structures. It is operated by Parks Canada. The commercial cruise ship *Kawartha Voyageur* carries passengers along the waterway, and several firms rent houseboats.

The Peterborough Lift Lock National Historic Site is located on the Otonabee River section of the Trent Canal in Peterborough. This massive concrete lock operates on a balance system that lifts boats 19.8 metres (65 ft) from lower to upper chamber. When it opened in 1904, the Peterborough Lift Lock was an engineering marvel, the highest lift lock in the world. After all these years, it's still fascinating to watch — even if you're not navigating the route aboard a cruise vessel or a vintage mahogany launch.

Things to See & Do

- Discover how to get from Lake Ontario to Lake Huron by water.
- Take a tour aboard the *Kawartha Voyageur*.
- Rent a houseboat with friends.
- Watch the Peterborough Lift Lock in action.

Parks Canada
2155 Ashburnham Drive
Peterborough ON
K9J 6Z6
705-750-4900
1-888-773-8888
pc.gc.ca/en/lhn-nhs/on/trentsevern

95

WASAGA BEACH PROVINCIAL PARK

~ Wasaga Beach

Wasaga Beach Provincial Park provides protective wildlife habitat for nesting shorebirds while also offering visitors some of the best lake swimming in Ontario.

At 14 kilometres (8.7 mi), Wasaga Beach is the longest freshwater beach in the world. Located at the southern tip of Georgian Bay, the fine-sand beach is divided into eight sections, and its sheltered position on the bay means that summer visitors can anticipate warm, shallow, clean water with great views of the Niagara Escarpment.

The park boasts 50 kilometres (31 mi) of hiking trails, the majority of

LEFT: Piping plovers require dry beaches for their eggs during nesting season, but rising water levels are submerging increasing amounts of beachfront. At Wasaga Beach, this at-risk species has found protected habitat. BELOW: Wasaga Beach is the longest freshwater beach in the world. Visitors can experience warm, shallow, clean water with great views of the Niagara Escarpment.

Wasaga Beach's Nancy Island Historic Site has a museum, theatre and replica lighthouse. On August 14, 1814, the island's namesake schooner, the HMS *Nancy*, engaged three American ships in a War of 1812 battle that helped define Canada's borders. Here, re-enactors replay that historical event.

which run through the dunes. The parts known as the "raised beaches" are actually remnants of a 10,000-year-old glacial lake. Many of the hiking and cycling trails are also open in winter, when they are cleared for cross-country skiing and snowmobiling. Wasaga's more than 30 kilometres (18.6 mi) of groomed trails offer some of the most enjoyable Nordic ski terrain in central Ontario, from the beginner-level Blueberry Trail to the advanced-level High Dunes Trail.

Wasaga Beach was the first provincial park in Canada to receive an international environmental "Blue Flag" designation for its careful management of the beach's fragile dune ecosystem. Of the park's 1,844 hectares (4,556 acres), 6.8 hectares (16 acres) have been designated "protected." The park is an important habitat for shorebirds, including the endangered piping plover, which returned to Wasaga in 2005 after a 30-year absence. At various times, some 230 species of birds populate the dune area. The high dunes are home to warblers, sparrows, woodpeckers and owls.

Wasaga Beach's Nancy Island Historic Site possesses a museum, theatre and replica lighthouse. On August 14, 1814, the island's namesake schooner, the HMS *Nancy*, engaged three American ships in a War of 1812 battle that helped define Canada's borders. The charred hull of the ship and artifacts from this key battle are proudly displayed. Summer visitors are invited to watch an award-winning video about the *Nancy*'s crew, tour the site, take part in musket and cannon demonstrations and meet historical re-enactors from Wasaga's past.

Things to See & Do

- Swim in the bay's warm, clear waters.
- Hike the high dunes trails.
- Watch the endangered piping plovers.
- Use some of the best Nordic ski trails in central Ontario.

General Information
11 22nd Street North
Wasaga Beach, ON
L9Z 2V9
705-429-2516
ontarioparks.com/park/
wasagabeach

96

KAKABEKA FALLS
～ Kakabeka Falls

Often referred to as the "Niagara of the North," 40-metre (130 ft) Kakabeka Falls — the second highest waterfall in Ontario — is located along the Kaministiquia River beside the village of Kakabeka Falls, 30 kilometres (19 mi) west of Thunder Bay. The name Kakabeka is said to be derived from the Ojibwe word *gakaabikaa*, meaning "waterfall over a cliff."

Centuries ago, the voyageurs used the Kaministiquia River as a major route to the northwest. They were the first Europeans to overwinter annually in northern Ontario. A 1.3-kilometre (0.8 mi) mountain portage was required to negotiate their massive canoes and weeks' worth of supplies around the falls.

The Kaministiquia River has cut deep into the Precambrian rock where Kakabeka Falls tumbles into the gorge below. The unstable shale lining the falls and the gorge has eroded to reveal fossils as old as 1.6 billion years, some of the oldest in existence. The rocks are also home to sensitive plant life, so visitors are prohibited from going into the gorge below the falls.

The 750-metre (0.5 mi) Boardwalk Trail offers excellent views of the falls and gorge, with viewing platforms on both sides. The boardwalk and pedestrian bridge are rated easy and wheelchair accessible. The slightly longer Mountain Portage Trail shares the same rating. This scenic trail traces a relatively level part of the historic portage route used by the voyageurs to traverse Kakabeka Falls. Little Falls Trail loop starts at Mountain Portage but descends steeply into the river valley to view picturesque Little Falls. Three other looped trails offer moderate-level hikes or, in winter, when the falls are spectacular, cross-country skiing.

Endangered lake sturgeon spawn at the base of the falls, and bald eagles congregate in the gorge below in the autumn when salmon make their run up the river to spawn.

The falls are part of the Ojibwe "Legend of Green Mantle," in which an Ojibwe chief, upon hearing of an imminent attack from an enemy Sioux tribe, instructed his daughter, Princess Green Mantle, to help devise a plan to protect her people. She entered the Sioux camp, pretending to be lost, and insisted that if they spare her life, she would take them to her father's camp. Placed in the bow of the canoe, she instead led the Sioux warriors over the falls to their deaths. According to the legend, Green Mantle can be seen in the mist of Kakabeka Falls. ～

Things to See & Do

- Experience the "Niagara of the North."
- Hike part of the historic voyageur portage route.
- Visit in the autumn during salmon run.
- Look for Princess Green Mantle in the mist.

General Information
P.O. Box 252
Kakabeka Falls, ON
P0T 1W0
807-473-9231
ontarioparks.com/park/kakabekafalls

BELOW: The "Niagara of the North," Kakebeka Falls is the second-highest waterfall in Ontario. It plummets 40 metres (130 ft) into the Kaministiquia River. FOLLOWING PAGES: The 750-metre (0.5 mi) Boardwalk Trail offers excellent views of the falls and gorge.

97 POLAR BEAR PROVINCIAL PARK

~ Hudson Bay

You'll probably never visit Polar Bear Provincial Park. It's an isolated, non-operational wilderness park in Ontario's far north. Its primary purpose — as its name implies — is the preservation of habitat for wildlife, particularly the 200 or more polar bear that migrate through the area seasonally. But Polar Bear Provincial Park helps give southerners a sense of just how big Ontario is.

When you're trapped in a routine weekday traffic jam on one of southern Ontario's 400-series highways, remind yourself that the province is actually 107,639,388 hectares (415,598 sq mi) of mostly wilderness and water. The "northern" city of Thunder Bay — 1,400 kilometres (870 mi) from Toronto — is still 830 kilometres (516 mi) south of Polar Bear Provincial Park. That's how big Ontario is.

Ontario's largest and most northerly park, Polar Bear lies on the western shore of Hudson Bay where it meets James Bay. It has no visitors' facilities and is accessible only by water or air. Landing permits must be obtained in advance for each of the park's four airstrips. There is little evidence of human presence in the park beyond an abandoned radar station — a few low metal buildings,

oil tanks, and some radio towers and radar dishes. But the barren Hudson Bay Lowlands landscape is ancient and remarkable.

The flattened terrain contains inland ridges that indicate former shorelines. Until about 4,000 years ago, the 450-million-year-old limestone bedrock was submerged beneath the Tyrrell Sea, the massive body of water that retreated to form Hudson and James bays. The part of the park located between the Canadian Shield and southern shores of Hudson Bay is a vast wetland, which often floods when the ice breaks up in late spring. The rest is part of the subarctic Hudson Plains, undisturbed low-lying tundra.

Subarctic conditions prevail. The treeline encircles the bays, dwindling north of the invisible limit. South of the treeline, stunted spruce, tamarack and willow brave the elements, while crowberry and mountain cranberry flourish. But in early summer, the tundra comes alive with colour — and nutrients. The park supports woodland caribou, moose, marten, fox, beaver, goose, black bear and polar bear. Some 200 polar bear wander the coastal areas in early November. Seals, walruses and belugas can be seen in coastal and estuarial waters.

Algonquian people lived here about 1,000 years ago, and their descendants, the present-day Cree, reside in the small coastal communities of Fort Severn and Peawanuck, just beyond the park's boundaries.

Though Polar Bear Provincial Park is strictly for wildlife, Wild Wind Tours, based in Peawanuck, offers guided eco-tours, photo tours and sportfishing tours along the shores of Hudson Bay, providing visitors with opportunities to see polar bear, whales, seals, caribou, waterfowl and more.

Things to See & Do

- Find Polar Bear Provincial Park on a map.
- Familiarize yourself with Ontario's northern limits.
- Read about the effect of climate change on northern wildlife.
- Consider an adventure with Wild Wind Tours.

Polar Bear
  Provincial Park
c/o Northeast Zone
  Office
P.O. Box 730
2 Third Avenue
Cochrane, ON
P0L 1C0
705-272-7107
ontarioparks.com/park/
  polarbear

98

SLEEPING GIANT PROVINCIAL PARK & OUIMET CANYON

～ Pass Lake

Sleeping Giant Provincial Park's namesake landform comprises mesas and sills that, when viewed from Thunder Bay, resembles a giant sleeping human. According to an Ojibwe legend, the giant is Nanabijou, who was turned to stone when he revealed the location of a rich silver mine (now known as Silver Islet) to European explorers. The thickest part of the giant's torso rises 563 metres (1,847 ft), and its cliffs, some reaching 250 metres (820 ft), are among the highest in Ontario.

The park occupies 24,346 hectares (60,160 acres) of the peninsula that forms the northwestern boundary of Lake Superior's Black Bay. It excludes the seasonal community of Silver Islet and a portion of Thunder Cape, at the peninsula's tip, which is designated as the Thunder Cape Bird Observatory.

The eastern portion of the park consists of lowlands, while the western half is composed of mesas, cliffs and valleys. Top of the Giant Trail, Head Trail and Thunder Bay Lookout offer breathtaking views of Lake Superior and its shores.

The park has more than 100 kilometres (62 mi) of trails suitable for both day and overnight hikes. You can hike the rugged shores of Lake Superior, past tower-

Ouimet Canyon is 100 metres (330 ft) deep, 150 metres (490 ft) wide and two kilometres (1.2 mi) long. A walkway consisting of boardwalks and trails leads to viewing platforms that overlook the canyon.

LEFT: The Sea Lion formation is a diabase dyke that has been left behind after the sedimentary rocks in which it crystallized eroded away. It juts out into Lake Superior at Perry Bay just northwest of Silver Islet. BELOW: The park offers amazing canoeing and kayaking opportunities. Northern Superior has some of the province's best sea-kayaking waters.

Things to See & Do

- Climb to the top of the Giant's head for spectacular views.
- Hike the 40-kilometre (25 mi) coastal Kabeyun Trail.
- Birdwatch at the Thunder Cape Bird Observatory.
- Take the walkway through Ouimet Canyon.

Sleeping Giant Provincial Park, RR 1 Pass Lake, ON P0T 2M0 807-977-2526 ontarioparks.com/park/ sleepinggiant ontarioparks.com/park/ ouimetcanyon

ing cliffs and up to the top of the Giant or venture to quiet lakes and streams deep within the park's wilderness areas. The 20 or so trails range in length from half a kilometre (0.3 mi) to the 40-kilometre (25 mi) Kabeyun Trail.

The shortest route to the top of the Giant's head is the aptly named one-kilometre Head Trail — a steep ascent delivers spectacular views. Another option is the challenging 2.7-kilometre (1.7 mi) Top of the Giant Trail. Once on top of the Giant, the trail takes hikers to scenic lookouts on both east and west sides of the peninsula. The 40-kilometre (25 mi) Kabeyun Trail requires overnight camping. This scenic coastal trail begins at Thunder Bay Lookout, rounds the tip of the peninsula, meanders over the boulders of a talus slope and ends at the trailhead at Highway 587. There are beautiful beaches and coves along the route.

There are excellent opportunities for wildlife sightings in the park's boreal forest, including moose, wolves, foxes and lynx. Over 200 bird species have been recorded, about 75 of which are known to nest in the park. These include a wide variety of songbirds, raptors, shorebirds and waterfowl.

In winter, Sleeping Giant offers some of the best cross-country skiing in Ontario, with 50 kilometres (31 mi) of groomed trails. The internationally recognized Sleeping Giant Loppet takes place on the first Saturday in March.

When you leave the Sleeping Giant, head east on the Trans-Canada Highway and watch for signs for Ouimet Canyon. Protected as part of Ouimet Canyon Provincial Park, the canyon is 100 metres (330 ft) deep, 150 metres (490 ft) wide and two kilometres (1.2 mi) long. A walkway consisting of boardwalks and trails leads to viewing platforms that overlook the canyon. Inside the canyon are rare alpine flowers and arctic plants normally found a thousand kilometres farther north.

99

TERRY FOX MEMORIAL & LOOKOUT

~ Thunder Bay

ABOVE: The Terry Fox monument is a bronze statue of Terry in motion. FACING PAGE: Today, more than 60 countries raise cancer research funds through the Terry Fox Run.

Things to See & Do

• Visit the statue and admire the man.
• Experience the view of Lake Superior.
• Learn more about a national hero.
• Go home and raise funds for a worthy cause.

Terry Fox Memorial
1000 Highway 11/17
Thunder Bay, ON
P7A 0A1
807-983-2041
1-800-667-8386
terryfox.org

Many of us have participated in the annual Terry Fox Run. It remains the world's largest one-day fundraiser for cancer research. To date, well over $650 million has been raised in Terry Fox's name. And we know a bit about this courageous young man from school lessons, travelling exhibits or from watching television coverage of his Marathon of Hope way back in 1980. But the sight of the statue created for the Terry Fox Memorial, in combination with the stunning view of Lake Superior from the Lookout, can be almost overwhelming: the spirit of one young, unyielding cancer victim versus the vastness of the land and the unknown.

Born in 1958, Fox was a distance runner and basketball player, a natural athlete. A diagnosis of osteosarcoma led to the amputation of his right leg in 1977, at the age of 19. Refusing to be defeated by disease, he continued to run, using an artificial leg, and played wheelchair basketball, winning three national championships.

In 1980, he attempted his historic cross-Canada run, the Marathon of Hope, to raise money for cancer research. His goal was to raise one dollar from each of Canada's 24 million residents. That April, he set out, westbound from St. John's, Newfoundland, with little media coverage. *How far could this kid go, realistically?* Each day, he ran the equivalent of a full marathon, and media coverage grew with his arrival at each new community along his route. By the time he reached Ontario, Terry Fox was a national hero.

After 143 days and 5,373 kilometres (3,339 mi), he was forced to end his run outside Thunder Bay. Cancer had spread to his lungs, and he died nine months later. Terry Fox did not beat cancer, and he did not live to finish his Marathon of Hope, but he did touch the hearts of millions worldwide. Today, more than 60 countries raise cancer research funds through the Terry Fox Run.

The monument, by sculptor Manfred Pervich, is a 2.7-metre (9 ft) bronze statue of Terry in motion atop a 45-ton granite base, with a foundation of local amethyst. While it is meant to symbolically mark the spot where Fox was forced to end his run on August 31, 1980, the actual terminus is roughly four kilometres (2.5 mi) to the west. But this location, with its quiet setting and commanding view over Lake Superior, is true to Terry Fox's heroic optimism and his perennial power to inspire us. ~

100 WABAKIMI PROVINCIAL PARK
~ Armstrong Station

Northwest of Lake Nipigon and Armstrong Station, Wabakimi Provincial Park is a true wilderness park situated entirely within the boreal forest. A massive expansion of the park in 1997 made it the second-largest park in Ontario (Polar Bear Provincial Park being the largest) and one of the world's largest boreal forest reserves.

The park is vast — 890,000 hectares (2.2 million acres) — with more than 2,000 kilometres (1,245 mi) of interconnecting lakes and rivers. As such, Wabakimi offers endless canoeing possibilities. Canoeists should be experienced, but suggested routes range from relaxing deep-woods paddling trips to adventurous encounters with world-class white water. It is interesting to note that two drainage basins divide along a high ridge, with the result that some of Wabakimi's waterways flow southeast toward the Atlantic Ocean via Lake Superior, while others flow north toward the Arctic Ocean via James Bay and Hudson Bay basins.

Things to See & Do

- Experience the true wilderness of the boreal forest.
- Canoe up to 2,000 kilometres (1,245 mi) of interconnected lakes and rivers.
- Discover ancient Aboriginal pictographs.
- Catch a glimpse of the elusive woodland caribou.

Ministry of Natural Resources/Parks
435 South James Street
Suite B001
Thunder Bay, ON
P7E 6S7
1-807-475-1321

The park contains more than 500 low-impact backcountry campsites (group size is limited to nine people), all of which are available on a first-come first-served basis; reservations are not required. Passes may be obtained either from the Parks Service or area outfitters.

Wabakimi Provincial Park is located on the traditional lands of several First Nations and Aboriginal communities. Pictograph sites found throughout the park suggest that Wabakimi has been inhabited for almost 7,000 years. One attraction was clearly the abundance of fish in its lakes and rivers, which remains the case today. Wabakimi boasts some of the best fishing in northwest Ontario, with abundant northern pike, perch, walleye, whitefish and lake trout. Other wildlife residents represent a who's who of the boreal forest: moose, woodland caribou, bear, timber wolf, lynx, fox, otter, muskrat, mink, weasel, marten, beaver and many smaller mammals.

The park offers a rare chance to see woodland caribou, now a vulnerable species. Only 300 or so roam Wabakimi, usually alone or in small groups. They are most often sighted along the shorelines of the park's lakes and rivers but are occasionally seen swimming across a lake.

Armstrong Station provides access points to Wabakimi, and the main line of the Canadian National Railway skirts the south end of the park, with Via Rail offering passenger service three times a week.

ABOVE: Wabakimi boasts some of the finest fishing in northwest Ontario, with abundant northern pike, perch, walleye, whitefish and lake trout. FACING PAGE: Wabakimi covers 890,000 hectares (2.2 million acres), with more than 2,000 kilometres (1,245 mi) of interconnecting lakes and rivers.

Acknowledgements

When I co-authored *Unforgettable Canada* with photographer George Fischer several years ago, I didn't envision a follow-up travel title. I would like to express my appreciation to Lionel Koffler, president, Firefly Books, for contacting me and suggesting this book project.

Tracy Read, my editor and confidante during the months it took to write *Unforgettable Ontario*, kept the train from derailing and the sky from falling. She not only worked with me on the text but kept track of the myriad details that assembling 100 trips create. Throughout, she was skilful, thoughtful and appropriately dark-humoured. Thanks, T.

Thank you to designer Janice McLean for making a busy book look calm. Selection and placement of images is a real art — particularly when the images are from a wide range of sources — and she kept the pages lively and cohesive. And thank you from all involved to Gillian Stead, who designed *Unforgettable Canada*, for allowing us to improvise with her original design. Thanks also to Firefly's George Walker for the book's maps and to Ella Galpern and Noor Majeed for their essential contribution to the photo research.

The following individuals kindly shared their photographs: Yvonne Brown, Prisca Campbell, Terry Culbert, Mary M. Derouard, Dudek Photography, Monica Evenden, Joe Gilker, Sarah Hogveen, Lisa Kwan, Bruce Laing, Paul and Soo Owens, Dave Pelaschak, James Roberts, Tony Saxon, Wil Wegman and Allen Woodliffe. Without their participation, this would have been a lesser book.

Also, thanks to the following larger entities for their generous contribution of images and information: the Aquatarium at Tall Ships Landing, Bata Shoe Museum, Canadian Canoe Museum, Canadian Museum of Nature, City of Owen Sound and Owen Sound Tourism, Collingwood Elvis Festival, The Corporation of Massey Hall & Roy Thomson Hall, The County of Prince Edward, Fergus Scottish Festival & Highland Games, Halton Radial Railway Museum, Headwaters Tourism, Hockey Hall of Fame, Huron County Museum & Historic Gaol, Jet Aircraft Museum, Kitchener–Waterloo Oktoberfest, London Children's Museum, Marmora SnoFest, McMichael, Canadian Art Collection, Municipality of Chatham–Kent, Museum London, Muskoka Steamships & Discovery Centre, Ontario Parks, Ontario Sea Kayaking Centre, Oxford County Tourism, Parks Canada, Pembroke Heritage Murals, Royal Agricultural Winter Fair, Royal Canadian Regiment Museum, Royal Ontario Museum, Science North, Sound of Music Festival, Stratford Festival and the City of Stratford, Tom Thomson Art Gallery, Town of Goderich, Town of Halton Hills, Town of Orangeville and The Word On The Street.

A big thank you to Ron Brown, Kevin Callan, Donna Carpenter, John DeVisser, Michael Gordon, Mark Harris, Liz Lundell, Greg McDonnell, Gary and Joanie McGuffin, James Raffan, Judy Ross, Nicola Ross, Donald Stanfield, and many other Boston Mills Press authors who taught me new things about Ontario.

And finally, thank you to my friend John Denison for driving me down half the back roads in the province and for helming Ontario publishing house Boston Mills Press for all those decades.

References

WEBSITES

activehistory.ca
agakhanmuseum.org
agawatrain.com
ago.net
algonquinpark.on.ca
baps.org
batashoemuseum.ca
bonnecherecaves.com
brockvilletourism.com
brucetrail.org
bushplane.com
canadaday.gc.ca
canadaslargestribfest.com
canadaswonderland.com
canadiangeographic.com
canoemuseum.ca
carnival.to
casaloma.ca
churchofourlady.com
circletrail.com
cityofwaterfalls.ca
cntower.ca
cobourgtourism.ca
conservationhamilton.ca

davidkjoyceminerals.com
discovermuskoka.ca
experience.simcoe.ca
fergusscottishfestival.com
forthenry.com
friendsoffortgeorge.ca
friendsofsandbanks.org
haliburtonsculptureforest.ca
haltonhills.ca/parks
headwaterscommunities.org
hhof.com
highpark.org
highparknature.org
hillsidefestival.ca
historicplaces.ca
lincoln.ca/content/balls-falls
londontourism.ca
manitoulin.ca
mariposafolk.com
marmorasnofest.ca
masseyhall.com
mcmichael.com
muralroutes.ca
nature.ca/en/home
niagarafallstourism.com

niagaragreenbelt.com
niagaraparks.com
niagarawinefestival.com
norfolktrails.ca
northernontario.travel
northfrontenac.com
oktoberfest.ca
ontarionature.org
ontarioparks.com
ontariossouthwest.com
ontariotrails.on.ca
ottawatourism.ca
pc.gc.ca
pembroke.ca/tourism
perth.ca
pridetoronto.com
prince-edward-county.com
rbg.ca
realmuskoka.com
rom.on.ca
roythomsonhall.com
saintemarieamongthe
   hurons.on.ca
saintgeorge.ca
soundofmusic.ca

stlawrencemarket.com
stratfordfestival.ca
terryfox.org
theex.com
thegreatwaterway.com
theismaili.org
thewordonthestreet.ca/
   toronto
todocanada.ca
todocanada.ca
town.bancroft.on.ca
tulipfestival.ca
uppercanadavillage.com
uwaterloo.ca/earth-sciences-
   museum
veg.ca/events/vegfoodfest
visitpec.ca
visitwindsoressex.com/
   riverwalk
wabakimi.on.ca
waterfallsofontario.com
wildwindtours.com
winecountryontario.ca
woodland-centre.on.ca

BOOKS

Bramble, Linda. *Touring Ontario's Wine Country*. Toronto: Lorimer, 2000.

Brown, Ron. *Backroads of Ontario*, 4th edition. Toronto: Firefly Books, 2016.

Brown, Ron. *Top 150 Unusual Things to See in Ontario*, 5th edition. Toronto: Boston Mills Press, 2016.

Byers, Mary, and John DeVisser. *Lake Simcoe and Lake Couchiching*. Toronto: Boston Mills Press, 2003.

Callan, Kevin. *A Paddler's Guide to Algonquin Park*. Toronto: Boston Mills Press, 2004.

Callan, Kevin. *A Paddler's Guide to Killarney and the French River*. Toronto: Boston Mills Press, 2006.

Dahms, Fred. *Picturesque Ontario Towns: Ten Daytrips in Eastern Ontario*. Toronto: Lorimer, 2003.

Dahms, Fred. *Wellington County*. Toronto: Boston Mills Press, 2008.

Denison, John. *Casa Loma and the Man Who Built It*. Toronto: Boston Mills Press, 1982.

Duke, A., and William Gray. *The Boatbuilders of Muskoka*. Toronto: Boston Mills Press, 2004.

Eagleson, Janet, and Rosemary Hasner. *Nature Hikes: Near Toronto Trails and Adventures*, rev. ed. Toronto: Boston Mills Press, 2009.

Earley, Chris, and Tracy C. Read. *100 Nature Hot Spots in Ontario: The Best Parks, Conservation Areas and Wild Places*. Toronto: Firefly Books, 2016.

Eyles, Nick. *Road Rocks Ontario: Over 250 Geological Wonders to Discover*. Markham: Fitzhenry and Whiteside, 2013.

Fischer, George, and Anthony Mollica. *Castles and Cottages: River Retreats of the Thousand Islands*. Toronto: Boston Mills Press, 2004.

Fischer, George, and Noel Hudson. *Unforgettable Canada: 115 Destinations*, 3rd edition. Toronto: Boston Mills Press, 2012.

Gordon, Michael. *Rockwatching: Adventures Above and Below Ontario*. Toronto: Boston Mills Press, 2005.

Harris, Mark, and George Fischer. *Ontario's Historic Mills*. Toronto: Boston Mills Press, 2007.

Harris, Mark, and George Fischer. *Waterfalls of Ontario*, 2nd edition. Toronto: Firefly Books, 2011.

Humphreys, Barbara, and Fiona Spalding-Smith. *Legacy in Stone: The Rideau Corridor*. Toronto: Boston Mills Press, 1999.

Lundell, Liz. *The Estates of Old Toronto*. Toronto: Boston Mills Press, 1997.

MacPherson, Allen. *Ontario Provincial Parks Trail Guide*, rev. ed. Toronto: Boston Mills Press, 2005.

McGuffin, Gary, and Joanie McGuffin. *Wilderness Ontario*. Toronto: Boston Mills Press, 2007.

Ross, Alec, and John DeVisser. *Kingston and Frontenac County*. Toronto: Boston Mills Press, 2009.

Ross, Nicola, and Gord Handley. *Caledon*. Toronto: Boston Mills Press, 1999.

Ross, Nicola. *Healing the Landscape: Celebrating Sudbury's Reclamation Success*. Sudbury: VETAC/COTMIV, 2001, 2008.

Runtz, Michael. *The Explorer's Guide to Algonquin Park*. Toronto: Boston Mills Press, 2000.

Runtz, Michael. *The Howls of August: Encounters with Algonquin Wolves*. Toronto: Boston Mills Press, 1997.

Stone, David. *Long Point: Last Port of Call*. Toronto: Boston Mills Press, 1988.

Stone, Kas. *Paddling and Hiking the Georgian Bay Coast*. Toronto: Boston Mills Press, 2008.

Tatley, Richard. *Segwun: A Muskoka Tour*. Toronto: Boston Mills Press, 1998.

Turner, Larry, and John DeVisser. *Rideau*. Toronto: Boston Mills Press, 1995.

Photo Credits

Index of Destinations

#		PAGE
20	Aga Khan Museum & Ismaili Centre l North York	58
75	Agawa Canyon Train Tour l Sault Ste. Marie	190
76	Algonquin Provincial Park & Barron Canyon l Algonquin Provincial Park	192
21	Art Gallery of Ontario l Toronto	60
37	Ball's Falls & Cataract Trail l Jordan/Ball's Falls	98
22	BAPS Shri Swaminarayan Mandir l Etobicoke	62
1	Basilica of Our Lady Immaculate & St. George's Anglican Church l Guelph	12
23	Bata Shoe Museum l Toronto	64
77	Beausoleil Island l Port Severn	196
78	Big Nickel, Dynamic Earth & Science North l Sudbury	198
2	Blue Mountain Resort & Collingwood Elvis Festival l Collingwood	14
55	Bon Echo Provincial Park & Mazinaw Rock l Near Kaladar	140
56	Bonnechere Caves & Fourth Chute Falls l Eganville	144
38	Brock's Monument & Historic Fort George l Queenston Heights	100
3	The Bruce Trail l Queenston–Tobermory	16
69	ByWard Market l Ottawa	172
70	Canada Day on Parliament Hill l Ottawa	174
39	Canada's Largest Ribfest vs. North America's Largest Vegetarian Food Festival l Burlington/Toronto	102
4	"Canada's Prettiest Town" & Its Historic Gaol l Goderich	18
40	Canada's Wonderland l Vaughan	104
79	Canadian Canoe Museum l Peterborough	200
71	Canadian Museum of Nature l Ottawa	176
24	Canadian National Exhibition & Royal Agricultural Winter Fair l Toronto	68
72	Canadian Tulip Festival l Ottawa	178
41	Canadian Warplane Heritage Museum l Hamilton/Mount Hope	106
25	Casa Loma & Spadina Museum l Toronto	70
26	Chinatown l Toronto	72
42	City of Waterfalls l Hamilton	108
5	"Classic Car Capital of Canada" l Chatham, Blenheim, Mitchell's Bay, Bothwell & Wallaceburg in Chatham-Kent	20
27	CN Tower l Toronto	74
43	Cobourg Beach & Sandcastle Festival l Cobourg	112
80	Cross-Country Skiing in Muskoka l Muskoka	202
28	The Distillery Historic District l Toronto	76
57	Family Day on the Waterway l Brockville	148
81	Fathom Five National Marine Park & Flowerpot Island l Tobermory	206
6	Fergus Scottish Festival & Highland Games l Fergus	22
82	French River Provincial Park l Alban	210
58	Fort Henry National Historic Site l Kingston	150
59	Fort Wellington National Historic Site & Battle of the Windmill National Historic Site l Prescott	152
7	Grand Bend Beach vs. Pinery Provincial Park l Lake Huron	24
83	Haliburton Sculpture Forest l Haliburton	214
44	Halton County Radial Railway Museum l Milton	114
45	Halton High Points l Mount Nemo, Rattlesnake Point, Kelso, Crawford Lake & Hilton Falls	116
29	High Park l Toronto	78
46	Hiking Headwaters Country l Erin, Caledon & Dufferin County	118
8	Hillside Festival l Guelph	28
60	Historic Perth l Perth	154
30	Hockey Hall of Fame l Toronto	80
84	Ice Fishing on Lake Simcoe l Lake Simcoe	216
96	Kakabeka Falls l Kakabeka Falls	240
85	Killarney Provincial Park & the La Cloche Mountains l Killarney	218
61	Kingston City Hall l Kingston	156
9	Long Point World Biosphere Reserve, Wildlife Area & Bird Observatory l Long Point	30
86	Manitoulin Island Indigenous Adventures l Manitoulin Island	220
87	Mariposa Folk Festival l Orillia	222
62	Marmora SnoFest & Sled-Dog Races l Marmora	158
31	Massey Hall & Roy Thomson Hall l Toronto	82
47	McMichael Canadian Art Collection l Kleinburg	122
10	Mennonite Country l St. Jacobs	32
88	"Mineral Capital of Canada" l Bancroft	224
89	Moose Safaris & Wolf Howls l Algonquin Park	226
11	Museums of London l London	34
90	Muskoka Steamships & Discovery Centre l Gravenhurst	228
48	Niagara-on-the-Lake Historic District & the Shaw Festival l Niagara-on-the-Lake	124
49	Niagara Falls l Niagara Falls	126
50	Niagara Wine Country & Wine Festivals l Niagara Peninsula	128
63	North Frontenac Dark Sky Preserve l South of Plevna	160
12	Oktoberfest l Kitchener–Waterloo	36
51	"Ontario's Best-Preserved Main Street" l Port Hope	130
13	"Ontario's Most Beautiful Village" l Elora	38
14	Oxford County Cheese Trail l Ingersoll, Woodstock & Bright	42
91	Paddlepalooza Kayak Festival l Parry Sound	230
64	Pembroke's Heritage Murals l Pembroke	162
92	Petroglyphs Provincial Park & National Historic Site l Woodview/Peterborough	232
15	Point Pelee National Park l Leamington	44
97	Polar Bear Provincial Park l Hudson Bay	244
52	Remembrance Park l Georgetown/Halton Hills	132
73	Rideau Canal National Historic Site l Ottawa–Kingston	182
16	Riverfront Trail & Sculpture Park l Windsor	48
53	Royal Botanical Gardens l Burlington	134
32	Royal Ontario Museum l Toronto	86
93	Sainte-Marie Among the Hurons National Historic Site l Midland	234
17	Salmon Tour & Tom Thomson Art Gallery l Owen Sound	50
65	Sandbanks Provincial Park l Prince Edward County	164
18	Six Nations of the Grand River l Ohsweken	52
98	Sleeping Giant Provincial Park & Ouimet Canyon l Pass Lake	246
54	Sound of Music Festival l Burlington	136
33	St. Lawrence Market l Toronto	88
19	The Stratford Festival l Stratford	54
99	Terry Fox Memorial & Lookout l Thunder Bay	248
66	The County l Prince Edward County	166
67	Thousand Islands National Park l St. Lawrence River	168
34	Toronto Caribbean Carnival Parade l Toronto	92
35	Toronto Pride Festival & Parade l Toronto	94
94	Trent–Severn Waterway & Peterborough Lift Lock National Historic Site l Trenton–Peterborough–Port Severn	236
68	Upper Canada Village l Morrisburg	170
100	Wabakimi Provincial Park l Armstrong Station	250
95	Wasaga Beach Provincial Park l Wasaga Beach	238
74	Winterlude l Ottawa	186
36	The Word On The Street l Toronto	96